HYPNOSIS
AND
DARK PSYCHOLOGY

How to Use Hypnosis Techniques to Analyze,
Influence and Persuade People. With Manipulation,
Brainwashing and Mind Control Secrets That
Only 1% of the Population Knows

By Scott Habits

validity or interim quality. Trademarks that are mentioned are done without written consent and can in no way be considered an endorsement from the trademark holder.

Table of Contents

Introduction

Have you ever wondered why it's difficult to listen to people sometimes? Or have you ever experienced having misunderstood what a friend or colleague told you? Learn how to develop and eventually master the art of listening! This lesson will allow you to discover the things which hinder you from actually hearing the messages being said. It will also enable you to be mindful of the emotions that possibly affect the way you perceive and receive things. It will especially be helpful in creating new relationships, rekindling acquaintances or re-establishing ties with co-workers or effectively addressing problems even in the family.

In hypnosis, words are everything. I know most of you will roll your eyes at the mention of hypnosis, thinking that it's all smoke and mirrors. But when used in the right way, in the right context, hypnosis can be one of the most powerful tools for self-improvement. Positive words are powerful. Try to remember a time when you felt good about yourself after having received praise and encouragement. Did it make you feel special? Did it inspire you to do even better? Did it improve your self-confidence? If you answered yes to all these, then you've just been a recipient of hypnosis!

Hypnosis isn't telling lies to make yourself feel good. It is about giving you courage and confidence to be your own best self. Words that we say to ourselves are like mental scripts that we have to recite because they dictate to a large degree our quality of life. They influence how we feel, what we are willing to do, and shows the limits to our potentials. Just as plays have scripts, these words serve as guides and "inner scripts" that make the difference in whether we choose to succeed or fail in life.

In this book, you will discover very powerful strategies that some of the world's most powerful hypnotists use to create the life they want. You will learn how to use these techniques on other people, and also on yourself to help you rise to the top in any part of your life. The great benefit here for you is these techniques seem so natural, no one will even know that you are using special mind hacking abilities to get what you want.

This book will give you the secret tools to connect with anyone in any situation. Perhaps you're in sales and need to persuade or convey a point to a prospect. Maybe you want to make more friends or develop deeper and more meaningful relationships with people. Perhaps you want to help others, or even help yourself get more of what you want. This book will provide you with the insight, tools, and wisdom to accomplish all of the above.

Each section of this book will cover tools and techniques you can start using right away on anyone and everyone; on family, friends, coworkers, spouses, business connections, prospects, etc.

When done correctly, hypnosis can be used to increase a person's self-esteem, heighten work productivity, treat phobias, and help them break away from bad habits. Hypnosis can also help a person lose weight, induce synesthesia, relieve stress—and a whole lot more!

When the mind is in a state of hypnosis, it becomes open to suggestion. You can embed an idea, an image, and even a memory into the human mind. By simply planting a suggestion into the subconscious, you can influence a person's behavior in real life.

This book contains proven steps and strategies on how to harness the power of hypnosis and to hypnotize anyone directly or indirectly through conversation.

You can use it to influence people to make deals go your way, it is ideal for use in business as well as in your personal life. Start to communicate better and have the upper hand in all conversations.

If you struggle with chatting up members of the opposite sex, change that right now. Know how to speak to people in such a way that they will be attracted to you, every time.

Chapter 1: Understanding Hypnosis

WHAT IS HYPNOSIS?

Hypnosis and mind control may seem like the same thing since they involve exerting control over someone else. However, there are glaring contrasts between the two. To recognize the distinctions, it is essential you become more acquainted with what they depend on.

Hypnosis is an artificially induced condition in which the individual reacts to inquiries or prompts from the hypnotist.

The procedure can be used on an individual or a gathering of people for a specific reason. At the point when this is utilized for therapeutic purposes, the process is known as hypnotherapy. In any case, when it is being used as a type of diversion for a crowd of people, it tends to be alluded to as organized hypnosis.

Mind control is the way of utilizing a few traps in getting the ideal response you need from others. You can use the secret to get command over what is happening in someone else's psyche. When it is utilized, it can enable you to center around the subject of your examination.

You can deal with your feelings and contemplations when you participate in this sort of reflection. As a rule, incredible people who accomplished extraordinary achievements in life could have ideal command over their psyches through daily reflection.

It is evident that hypnosis and mind control have clear contrasts. A few components utilized in one may likewise be used in the other, but they are not the same. Everything relies upon how you are ready to draw in the essential standards included.

You have heard of hypnosis. You have surely seen it used on television where the hypnotist tells the person they are getting sleepy. They usually swing some type of pendulum in front of them and then the person falls asleep, completely under the control of the hypnotist. While it happens a bit differently in real life, the end result is the same. Once you can successfully hypnotize people, you can control what they do and think.

Once a person is under hypnosis, you can make suggestions. For example, you want a person to buy you something. You hypnotize them and suggest they buy it for you. Once they come out of the hypnosis, chances are they will get you what you suggested in the very near future.

Now, when you are using hypnosis in this way, you want to do it without the person knowing you are. You will not swing in a pendulum in front of their face to induce the trance state.

DEMYSTIFYING HYPNOSIS

Hypnosis is not about making you bark like a dog or cluck like a chicken. It is not about enslaving you under the control of some Svengali who has enraptured you and now will make you do what they want. In truth, hypnosis is about connecting you with your unconscious mind, giving you greater freedom and personal power to transform your life. Every day you experience trance. Whether you are driving home and suddenly look around and do not know how you got home. Alternatively, you sat down in front of the television with Netflix on and suddenly looked up and realized the sun had gone down and you have been sitting there all day.

Maybe you believe that you are bad at math, that you get anxious when something happens, or when your anxious food is a great relaxing thing for you. These are all suggestions and trances that have been embedded into your unconsciousness throughout your life. Hypnotic programming informs in your life, even though you may have never thought you have been hypnotized.

Your brain works on an unconscious and a conscious level. Your consciousness is your gatekeeper; it has a very limited ability to help you make changes, mostly because your conscious mind does not require a lot to get overloaded. It is great in helping you make a decision, on the self-talk that you do, and other such things. But, the very act of you moving your hands requires so many muscles and nerves to fire, so many structural fibers that you, if you were to consciously try to do it, would be impossible. The human foot makes a series of micro-adjustments as a person stands and walks that we have yet been able to replicate in anything and all of that is done in the unconscious. Your unconscious mind manages almost everything else in your life.

Every second your unconscious brain processes twenty million bits of information, the conscious mind only processes about forty bits of information and that is why hypnosis is so powerful. Our habits, our beliefs, our world outlook, all of these things are embedded in our unconscious mind. How we believe things, why we believe things, how we act on our beliefs, all of these are unconscious. In fact, some studies suggest that even large parts of what feels like conscious decision making happen unconsciously before they happen consciously. Think about that. What we perceive as a free choice, is oftentimes, a completely unconscious process that we rationalize as a free choice afterward. And to many people, when they hear that, it sounds scary. It might make them even question their view of who they are or what freedoms they have. But to those who understand hypnosis, it offers an opportunity for them to create massive change that they will be able to enjoy and reap the benefits of with ease.

Through hypnosis, a person is often guided into their unconscious and able to layer their desired changes into their unconscious so that they can more easily make changes.

But, you might be wondering, you have seen people clucking like a chicken and barking like a dog. You have maybe watched people or heard about people who forgot their name or danced like a stripper. So what was going on there if hypnosis is just about relaxation, visualization, and mental programming for positive change? Is everyone just pretending? Is it all just fake? Well, the answer is no.

Stage hypnosis relies on people's general ability to want to do crazy things. It uses social pressure and compliance and proper selection to create a compelling display of hypnotic showmanship. The stage hypnotist does a hypnotic test with the audience for anyone that wants to participate and then chooses those who are most responsive. Then when they are on stage, he begins to run them through a series of hypnotic tests, eliminating one person after another who is not fully responding to the hypnotic suggestions that they are putting out there, until all they have on stage is a group of people willing and able to follow directions. And here is the thing, you might have been one of these people, or you have witnessed a friend of yours do it. You might say to yourself that they swear on a stack of bibles that they were hypnotized and I would say that was 100% true.

The thing is though that what is really happening is that the people on stage have given themselves the permission to be hypnotized and in so doing have abdicated their responsibility to someone else. In 1963 Stanley Milgram wanted to test people's compliance to find out if Nazism was a German weakness, or if people, when faced with authority, could be pushed to do horrible things. Volunteers were told they were doing a study on memory and they were to administer an electric shock to another volunteer if they got the question wrong. At each point, the shocks would increase in intensity. The thing was that everyone except the volunteer was an actor and no one was receiving electric shocks. As they went through the process, a doctor in a white coat would simply insist that they keep going; they keep doing what needs to be done. Each time, people bowed to authority, especially as they were consistently told that the doctor would take full responsibility. Stage hypnosis works in exactly the same way. They are going along because they can go along because they know that no matter what they do, they have someone they can blame it on. That means they are empowered.

Is hypnosis just a benign thing? The answer here is very mixed. The fact is that hypnosis is a tool, like any other tool, and it can be made a weapon. The thing is that almost nobody knows how to do it and anything you could do in hypnosis to someone, you could do without hypnosis 100x easier. But, of course, hypnosis is powerful. It is after all capable of having you transform your unconscious mind and plant new thoughts, ideas and beliefs inside of it.

Hypnosis is one of the most unique phenomena that only now with the breakthrough technology in brain scans are we even beginning to see any major understanding of. We know now that it transforms the way people think and process information. Where we are usually responding to stimulation (see food and thus want to eat it), instead, when a person has been hypnotized, they act out their thoughts first (meaning if they are on a diet, they do not respond to the food). This may sound like a small change, but it is not. A powerful transformation makes a person self-directed in their life, given the ability to decide what actions they take, rather than simply being drawn to something form their unconscious programming.

And the best thing about hypnosis is that it is not very difficult to learn. Neither self-hypnosis nor the hypnotic protocols on other people. All of which, you are about to learn.

STAGES OF HYPNOSIS

There are four stages all people go through when you are working to get to their unconscious mind:

- **Stage One:** You have to make sure that you have their undivided attention.
- **Stage Two:** You have to get them to a state of compliance.
- **Stage Three:** You have to activate their unconscious response.
- **Step Four:** They are now under your control and you simply need to lead them to the outcome you desire.

PRINCIPAL COMPONENTS OF HYPNOSIS

Hypnosis includes two principal components: acceptance and proposals. Trancelike acceptance is the major proposal conveyed amid the procedure of hypnosis; however, what it should comprise of is a matter of discussion.

Proposals are commonly communicated as suggestions that inspire automatic reactions from the members, who don't trust they have much or any control over the circumstance. A few people are likewise more susceptible than others, and specialists have discovered that these individuals are more likely to have a decreased feeling of authority while under hypnosis.

Susceptibility to hypnosis has been characterized as the capacity to encounter proposed modifications in physiology, sensations, feelings, musings or conduct. Neuroimaging procedures have demonstrated that these individuals show higher activity levels in the prefrontal cortex, foremost cingulate cortex, and parietal systems of the mind amid various periods of hypnosis.

These are regions of the mind associated with a scope of complex capacities, including memory and observation, feelings and assignment learning. Be that as it may, the particular cerebrum components associated with hypnosis are as yet hazy. However, researchers are starting to sort out the neurocognitive profile of this procedure.

How would you know whether somebody has been hypnotized? Various changes indicate that the subject is in a hypnotic trance. NLP calls these profound daze markers, and they are a set of highly detailed observations one can make of the subject. Recognizing such markers requires practice and focus. And not all of these markers need to be present to establish that a subject is under hypnosis.

BECOMING A HYPNOTIC PERSON

What does it mean to become a hypnotic person? This is actually fairly easy. Unlike hypnosis itself, being a hypnotic person is about being present with people around you. The more you are out of your head, the more hypnotic you become to everyone else around you. Most people walk through life, waiting for their turn to speak, and listening to people just enough to know what they can say or should say. A truly hypnotic person instead is a lover of people, a listener, someone who finds them to be interesting and worthy of their attention. When you give a person that level of attention, you make them feel as if they are important. When you make a person feel like they are important, they want to go out of their way for you and they feel attracted to you. Because people like those who make them feel special.

Now, there is a difference from making a person feel special and treating someone as special and this is a mistake many people make on their journey to be a hypnotic person. Hypnotic people are not trying to get something from someone, so at the same point, they do not need to impress them, and they are indifferent to their opinions of them. No, a hypnotic person simply cares enough about people to listen to them... really listen to them, and to take an interest in them.

Once you have mastered the ability to truly listen and hear what someone has to say, then you are left with your eye contact and your touch. A hypnotic person uses eye contact constantly. They are not gawkers; they do not sit there and just stare at someone. No, but, when they are listening to the person, when the person is talking, their eyes are on them. One of the most powerful things you can remember to do is to stare at someone right at the bridge of their nose. It builds a tunnel vision and creates a link between you and the person you are talking with.

Hypnotic people are masters at the eyebrow raise. This simple gesture, you have probably done a hundred times. You see someone you know or someone you are waiting for, you look at them, they look at you, your eyebrows raise, and your head slightly nods. This has been called many things by many gurus, the hypnotic hello, the eyebrow flash, and the such... but whatever you want to call it; this is a hugely effective way to capture someone's attention from across the room. And it is another powerful tool for the hypnotic person.

All in all, when you want to be a hypnotic person, it is about getting out of your own head, and being fully present at the moment. This more than all the other techniques are worth repeating because everything else will come from this. Your life will transform when you do this. And the way people respond to you will transform as well.

THE DARK SIDE OF HYPNOSIS

Surely, we are not being hypnotized and brainwashed in this modern age? Yes, we are… more than ever. Today's government has so much control over us through the devious use of hypnotic propaganda, that we don't know what is true. The government tells the major media outlets what to print just to get a reaction that benefits them and furthers their agenda. On any given day you will see the same lead story on the front page of every major newspaper. People are hypnotized by their smart phones, so much so that you can see a video of people falling into open manholes while gazing intently at their phones. Usually, If they're not immersed in the activity on their phones then they are staring droopy eyed at a computer monitor with their mouths hanging open. Facebook is keeping them hypnotized. The internet is the ultimate hypnotic tool for the government to use to enforce its will and keep people nice and calm. We don't want any revolutions, right? The sad part of all of this government control is that we, the citizens, are allowing it to happen. It's not totally fair to blame the citizens for falling prey to the hypnotic trap though; after all, we have been hypnotically programmed since we entered preschool to fall into line. Nowadays, we actually invite a hypnotic device like, Amazon's Alexa machine, into our homes so the government can listen to and record our private conversations.

HYPNOTISM IS REAL

Simply put, it is the ability to make suggestions to someone that filter through deep layers of their consciousness. This ability to make deep, impactful suggestions to someone while they are in a vulnerable and suggestible state grants hypnotic dark manipulators a high level of power over their victims. Unlike almost every other technique in this book, hypnotism is not something that people encounter in a milder, more innocent form in their day-to-day lives.

Hypnotism can take the form of both verbal and nonverbal suggestive practices. Often, the forms of suggestion are very subtle and therefore difficult to detect. By its very nature, hypnosis works on the deepest levels of a person's mind. Someone who is skilled in generating a hypnotic state and response in someone will be able to bypass their defenses and influence them without raising any alarms or giving a person a chance to raise their guard.

What people describe as hypnosis has two key traits: automaticity and responses feeling very real to the hypnotized subject. Automaticity is where responses that occur feel to the subject that they occurred without their conscious involvement, like swatting a fly away from your face without thinking about it and feeling like it happened automatically. The other key trait, responding to suggestions or ideas with the response feeling very real to the subject would have for example, a subject being told they can't stand up and they accept this idea then the idea that they can't stand up will feel very real to them, no matter how much they want to stand and try to stand, they won't be able to do so. They may be thinking that they don't believe this will work, they don't believe they are hypnotized and they believe they will be able to stand, but this doesn't change the perceived reality of the situation they have found themselves in.

You may be thinking at this point "isn't hypnosis about increasing suggestibility so that people do as you tell them?" This is a common myth. Hypnotizing someone doesn't increase their suggestibility. The very slight increase in suggestibility in some people is thought to be due to other everyday ordinary factors. Hypnosis is a natural phenomenon

If people are role-taking it wasn't thought that this was something they were consciously deciding to do, but instead a role they were taking on implicitly from the context, the overt instructions of the hypnotist and the hypnotist's non-verbal communication. Just like when you are in the presence of a parent you take on the role of son or daughter, when you are in the presence of a teacher, you take on the role of student, and when you are in the presence of a doctor you take on the role of patient. You don't consciously decide to take on these roles, or any other role in life, you take on these roles naturally and throughout life most people learn to take on different roles for different situations. They don't enter the situation thinking about getting into character, it happens automatically, so it may be with hypnosis. That those who expected that they are supposed to be more suggestible during hypnosis responded quicker to suggestions within hypnosis, those who didn't know either way didn't increase or decrease their suggestibility, and those who thought only weak-willed people could be hypnotized, or had some negative thoughts towards hypnosis perhaps, became less suggestible and took longer to respond to suggestions.

It could be that there is a memory consolidation and learning interplay between the two types of sleep, where the brain is updated with the new learning and memories during NREM sleep by stimulating the same neural pathways involved at the time of learning.

WHAT MAKES SOME PEOPLE MORE HYPNOTIZABLE THAN OTHERS?

The latest thinking on why some people seem to be more hypnotizable than others is around the functional communication between an individual's salience and executive control networks, or the attentional network. The greater the connectivity the more hypnotizable the individual. The executive network is involved in decision-making, planning, paying attention and working memory. The salience network is involved in selecting what internal and external stimuli we should be attending to at any given moment.

The perceptual system involves perceiving the world around you and interpreting that to decide how you should respond, this includes stereotypes and mimicking behaviors (rapport), and is processed not just with the observed stimuli but also internal meaning is activated. The perceptual system is always monitoring the environment at a preconscious level to help you know how to respond to different things in the environment. This can lead directly to behaviors, or it can pass through the evaluative system, evaluating the perceptions before leading to behaviors and the motivational system can feed into the perceptual system before leading to behaviors also.

As mentioned, the evaluative system deals with approach or avoid evaluation. This can lead directly to behavior, or it can feed in to the motivational system and then to behavior, creating a stronger response, or the motivational system can feed into the evaluative system before leading to behaviors. This system helps us respond to whether an environmental stimulus is good or bad without having to think about it, like whether we should approach and pick one berry over a different berry elsewhere.

Strong emotion takes too long to develop to be totally non-conscious because it requires many changes throughout the body. What is thought happens with emotion, for example with fear, is that you are in a situation and something gives you a sense that the situation may be dangerous and fear emotion begins in your body. Only a small amount of this feeling is needed to lead to automatic behavior to run away before you consciously process why you are feeling fear and running away. But often the fear feeling continues for a while after the incident because it takes time for the full feeling of fear to develop and then the biological changes don't suddenly dissipate, so you link this with the event and then with thinking about the event just after it has ended and this then strengthens the learning to respond in this way in the future.

If the event was an innocent event, like walking along a country path pushing aside branches, and then one branch that is pushed aside ends up flicking a spider in your face, you don't have time to behaviorally respond based on an emotion because the event happened too quickly for an emotional reaction. So another system would lead to the automatic response of jumping, likely the evaluative system, but at the same time fear emotion would begin, this would impact on cognition and updating memories with the fear emotion to be scared of spiders, or perhaps scared to be pushing through trees like that again in the future, or even scared of anything which may remind you of this incident happening.

WHAT ABOUT HYPNOTHERAPY?

When hypnosis is used to deal with health issues it is called hypnotherapy. Hypnosis is about guiding trance and interacting with the non-conscious with hypnosis a therapist guides the client's attention and is communicating with the client's whole brain, they may be consciously aware of what you are saying and doing but the communication isn't aimed at the conscious awareness. Many of the indirect hypnotic techniques communicate and interact directly with the client on a non-conscious level often bypassing their conscious awareness.

So, one reason you use hypnosis is that it goes beyond the narrow band of conscious awareness and the limitations that this entails with trying to access information and understandings which often we have very little to no real access. Often interpretations we may make are guesses, which may or may not be accurate, and trying to put everything that makes up the problem and solution into words and to express it satisfactorily is almost impossible to do.

Chapter 2: What Is Dark Psychology?

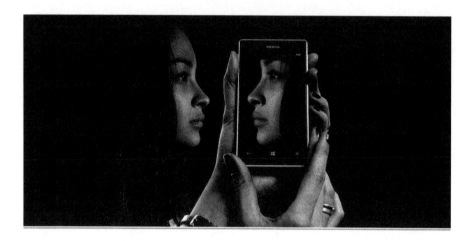

Dark psychology is about using the mental weaknesses that people have to get people to do what you want them to do. The fact is that everywhere around the tools of dark psychology are chipping away at your mind. Dark Psychology is about recognizing the compulsions, needs, and desires that we all have and that can be used to get what we want.

You have desires and wants, you have needs, and how far are you willing to go to have those things met. Do you know? What are your buying triggers? What are your emotional triggers? You have them but are you completely aware of them. What makes you stressed, confused, angry, happy, and excited? All of these things are inside your mind? They are inside everyone's mind. And when you know how to access them, in yourself and in others, suddenly you will have greater freedom, happiness, excitement, and possibility. Because finally, you will be bringing your desires to life, by getting others to see and want to help.

Dark Psychology is a tool, like a hammer. You can use it to build things or you can use it as a weapon to hurt people. The world can be a dangerous place. Knowing these techniques and knowing how people can manipulate you or try to, will fundamentally transform the way you respond to people and how you engage with them. You will be able to recognize when people are trying to use your emotional states and when they are trying to take advantage of you. You will also learn how to use these techniques in ethical ways so that you can guide people to take the best action for themselves or the action you think they should take. Beyond everything, you will discover through dark psychology what exactly is triggering your behaviors and in part two, how to change those triggers if they aren't helpful or serve you in the way that you want them to.

Have you ever pondered on the inner workings of the minds of certain heinous criminals or those everyday people who display some deviant characters? You may have asked yourself what they feel, think, or the motivation behind their actions. Do they feel pity or regret? These questions and many others like them are what propelled, and still moves, the study of dark psychology. This part of our psyche is not so separate from our beliefs, faith, goals, ideologies, and culture. In fact, some of the most criminal and horrid behaviors have often originated from them. But dark psychology makes the point that these actions may not, and quite often do not, have any particular goal.

Usually, when an individual goes out of their way to victimize or manipulate someone else, the drive behind such actions is money, vengeance, sex, love, or power. This type of behavior can be easily understood, as most of us can relate to such emotions. But there are those whose motivation does not come from any of those driving factors. They hurt, kill, and manipulate people just because. This inherent darkness or evil, as some would term such actions, is present in the psyche of every human being, whether in times past or in our modern society. There are no exceptions. This nature, latent or manifested to cause harm to those who have done us no wrong, is a very complex study indeed, but one which must be undertaken for the purpose of the continuous flourishing of society.

The human condition related to the psychodynamics of those who prey upon others in a way that is motivated by deviant methods is known as dark psychology. Throughout this book, you will be studying bits of dark psychology because it can help you further understand mind control and how it works.

Virtually every human has the ability to tap into dark psychology. This may sound somewhat terrifying, since dark psychology is often known to be the psychology fostered by psychopaths and sociopaths, and it can be the entire foundation for how many major crimes are committed. However, in this book, you will learn about dark psychology and how you can use it to your benefit without compromising your own wellbeing, as well as how you can use the understanding of dark psychology to prevent yourself from being brainwashed by others.

The majority of dark psychology is based on goal-oriented motivation that can be rationalized by the individual who is completing the activities. Dark psychology includes the thoughts, feelings, and perceptions fostered by those who are responsible for using dark psychology to complete certain actions.

A lot of the forms of mind control are considered to be rooted in dark psychology because many believe that mind control is an impure strategy used by those who cannot be bothered to do things themselves. They believe that it is a form of evil, hence why it is called "dark" psychology. While we certainly do not want to alleviate the blame from true criminals, you should understand that you are not a criminal for using mind control strategies.

Mind control in this day and age can be a powerful way to encourage people to do the things you need or want them to do. Obviously, this type of powerful strategy can be used to have people do bad things or to create criminal results, but it can also be used to encourage positive results. The way this method works for you is entirely up to you. If you choose to use these strategies to justify and execute criminal behaviors, then you will become a criminal and you will likely end up prosecuted as such.

However, if you use these strategies to benefit yourself and those around you without doing harm to anyone, then there truly is nothing wrong with using mind control to get what you want. Many people who use mind control for various purposes, such as selling, building businesses, encouraging employees to do what they should be doing to keep a business running well, encouraging people to see past their fears and limitations, and much more. Being able to control someone's mind leaves you with a lot of power to do many positive things. Just as much power as you have to do evil things, even. How you choose to use your skillset is entirely up to you.

DARK PSYCHOLOGY IN MODERN TIMES

As society continues to move forward technologically, this progressiveness affects how we deal with each other. People who seek to violate others would employ these new means to achieve their nefarious goals. The internet is one of the biggest and most influencing new age developments. With little more than a few clicks, people from different countries would find themselves connected. This has been a positive innovation. But it was only a matter of time until such individuals as pedophiles, fraudsters, and other criminal personalities found that the internet made things much easier for them. A new set of nefarious characters also emerged as the internet grew and became more accepted; hackers.

Despite the massive body of work on dark psychology, it is still relatively unknown today. Psychologists and similar professionals may be knowledgeable on the subject, but this knowledge is not commonplace. The realm of dark psychology is not one that anybody should be ignorant of. This region of our minds is home to some of our most extreme evil and also of our most desirable qualities, as we will learn when we discuss shadow. As emotional intelligence and self-discovery continue to be championed above IQ in recent times, we must also ask ourselves the necessary questions. This would, ultimately, uncover all that hides in those darkest and most secretive recesses of our consciousness.

Chapter 3: How Hypnosis Works

Hypnosis is a state of receptivity. When a person is in hypnosis, they are more open to suggestions and messages given by the hypnotist. The suggestions, within reason, are not analyzed by the conscious mind, but they are accepted by the subconscious mind. Once messages go into the subconscious mind, they become automatic and natural responses.

This altered state happens naturally throughout the day. Anytime you zone out, daydream, or even go into a deep state of focused concentration; you go into a state similar to hypnosis! You also pass into a hypnotic state as you are falling asleep at night, and when awakening in the morning. The average person does not know that they are more receptive as they are waking up or falling asleep, so they usually overlook the benefits of using these naturally occurring receptive states. It is a fact that once an idea gets implanted into the subconscious mind, it stays there until a new one replaces it. The longer an idea remains in your subconscious mind, the harder it becomes to replace it with a new one.

THE PROCESS OF HYPNOSIS STRIVES TO UNLOCK YOUR SUBCONSCIOUS MIND

This is how hypnosis works. It attempts to replace your old thought patterns with new ones to change the basic way your subconscious and the conscious mind works.

Hypnosis works by bringing the action of this subconscious to the forefront and gives the control of our conscious mind the backseat. It clears all the clutter that might cloud your conscious mind and makes way for the subconscious to accept new thoughts and ideas.

THE CONSCIOUS AND SUBCONSCIOUS MIND

For you to be able to understand how to hypnotize someone, it's first important to know that the concept of hypnosis is entirely based on the intricate relationship between the conscious and subconscious mind.

In our daily lives, we seem to be in total control of our conscious minds. In other words, it appears to us that we use our conscious minds to think and make decisions. Meanwhile, we tend to think of our subconscious mind as a dormant part of our brain, not having much to do with our everyday functioning.

However, the opposite is true. It is actually the subconscious mind that controls the actions of our conscious mind. In fact, our subconscious mind is the most automatic part of our brain, the one which controls most of our life processes including emotions, reflexes, automatic behavior, belief systems and even breathing. Above all, our subconscious mind is responsible for how we perceive the world around us, how our body processes the physical information it receives and how our key thought processes are formed.

To see how the conscious and subconscious mind differ as well as relate to each other, you can compare your brain to the functioning of a computer. While your conscious mind works according to the Central Processing Unit (CPU), it is your subconscious mind that actually functions as the hard drive. Your subconscious mind holds all the patterns and ways according to which your conscious mind will react to life around you. Your subconscious mind is going through constant changes or 'reprogramming', through the situations, events, people and happenings around you.

Hypnosis works by changing this programming of the subconscious mind and allowing it to change how your conscious mind behaves. The subconscious mind equates for 90% and the conscious mind 10%.

You must understand the difference between conscious communication and subconscious communication. The conscious part of the mind is a very analytical, logical, critical part of the mind where information is analyzed. However, to change a person's habits, patterns, beliefs, feelings, sensations, emotions, etc., we want to get into the subconscious part of the mind. We do this by bypassing the conscious, analytical, critical mind. The way that you'll be learning how to do this is with hypnotic communication will allow you to connect with anyone hypnotically so what you say will bypass the critical mind and get directly into the powerful and natural subconscious mind.

Think about a person you spend time with, and every time you're around them, they have this natural ability to lift your spirits and put you in a great mood. On the opposite end of that, there are people you associate with that we called a fun sponge. They seem to suck all the fun, happiness, and joy out of even the best of situations. Wouldn't it be great to be the person who can positively impact a person's state of mind, mood, and emotional state? Using this form of hypnotic communication, you'll be able to do precisely that.

Conscious Versus Subconscious Communication

The conscious mind is the very logical and analytical part of the mind. The last thing you want is for your target to be analyzing every word that comes out of your mouth. The more people overanalyze what you are saying, the more they have a chance to build doubt, fear, resistance, and objections against you. The subconscious is the part of the mind that stores all of your experiences and also composes your thoughts, feelings, emotions, behaviors, feelings, and habits. We want to communicate with that part of the mind so we can bypass any analytical thinking, knock down any resistance, and build trust with our target. When you communicate directly to the subconscious mind, the target is more likely to accept what you say as the truth because you are evoking emotions, feelings, and sensations that can influence their behaviors, habits, and decisions. That can be used in any sales situation or relationship.

Upon first learning how to connect with someone hypnotically, sometimes people think they will use their voice or their words to zap a person into a trance. However, there is much more than just hypnotic language, although you will learn a lot of hypnotic language in this book. The words we speak only forms 7% of the way we communicate. The other 93% comprises nonverbal communication. Much of this is in body language. You can tell a lot about a person by their posture, their gestures, the way they move their hands, and even their eye movement.

THE CRITICAL FACTOR

In your pursuit of learning how to hypnotize someone, you will need to master the art of bypassing the critical factor in your subject's mind.

The critical factor is a part of the conscious mind which stands like a filter between it and the subconscious. It has the ability to accept or reject any new stimulus, such as ideas or thoughts that might want to enter your conscious mind from the subconscious. The basic duty of the critical factor is to protect our minds from any threats and dangers. By design, our nervous system views change and new ideas as a threat. Hence, any new stimulus is not likely to be seen as a part of our existing mental set-up. As a result, the critical factor rejects such inputs from the subconscious, thus preventing change.

The process of hypnosis helps to quiet down the critical factor for a short while, clearing the way for passage of new ideas from the subconscious to the conscious mind.

BYPASSING THE CRITICAL FACTOR

How to communicate to the subconscious mind is through a process called "bypassing the critical factor of the conscious mind." The critical factor is like a filter that keeps information from getting to the subconscious mind unless it belongs there. Five basic principles bypass the critical factor. When this filter is bypassed (or lowered), it can form new habits or programs, evoke emotional states, or influence a belief or the way we perceive something. I often hear people express concerns that their "guard will be lowered," and are often afraid that the result can be catastrophic; however, our critical factor is bypassed naturally every day through many sources. Let's get into the most common ways to bypass this mechanism, or "lower the guard," so that you can be aware of them, and how to use these principles in your communication.

These five ways to bypass the critical factor are:

1. **Heightened Emotional States**

Anytime you experience a heightened emotional state, your guard is lowered, and information naturally enters the subconscious mind. This is often how fears and anxieties form. Fear is a heightened emotional state where a person can experience a fight or flight response. Negative emotions will usually result in a negative mismatched program that forms.

For example, someone may be anxious when they walk into a sales presentation even though they know there is no reason for them to be afraid. This could stem from when that person was a child and got criticized in a classroom, and that mental program could have been generalized to all presentations or situations where they must talk in front of people.

In the same way that negative emotions bypass the critical factor of the conscious mind to form new programs, positive emotions will have a similar effect. When people experience positive emotions though, they will often feel good about the decisions they are making, and the people around them. Therefore, it is crucial that in your communication strategies, to build the "know, like and trust factor," you evoke positive emotions in your target. Imagine if you are selling your services or product to them, and they are feeling happy and excited about it, they will feel much better about listening to you, and the resistance goes down. When you evoke positive emotions, you can also get people to make decisions faster and easier, feel better about the decision they are making, and have their choice benefit both you and them.

2. <u>Repetition Is the Mother of All Learning</u>

You may have heard this before: "repetition is the mother of all learning." This statement is true. Every time something is repeated, it knocks on the critical factor until it lowers that guard and gets into your subconscious mind. That is why advertisers say it takes 7 to 11 repetitions of a message for a target or prospect to take action or decide about the product. Think about things you just do naturally, habits or behaviors you have that you don't even have to think about anymore. Brushing your teeth, tying your shoes, opening a door, driving a car. You don't have to sit there every time you open a door and analyze how to do it, do you? Of course, not! You have repeated that action or behavior so often that it becomes a natural part of your powerful subconscious mind. That is why you should use the repetition of a message when communicating with your target. Often, people will misinterpret this principle and think they must repeat the same sentence or phrase repeatedly, but you don't have to use the same sentence or phrase over again, you can use the repetition of a concept or idea conveyed in different ways.

Think of jingles or product slogans you hear on the radio or television. As soon as a commercial play, they have a jingle associated with a particular product so when you hear the jingle, you think of the product. That is due to having listened to that jingle several times. That is also why in commercials and advertisements you will often hear phone numbers, websites, or services repeated at least three times. It creates a link in your memory with the information they want you to record and remember.

3. **Authority and Credibility**

There are just some people that we build such a high level of respect or trust in that everything they say is held in high regard. That is often true with religious figures. When people enter a church, synagogue, temple, or any other religious institution, our critical factor becomes bypassed. The same thing is valid with parents, coaches, doctors, and some political figures. Without getting controversial here, if you want to see a great example of mass hypnosis, the next time you walk into a church, and everyone stands and sings at the same time, ask yourself "Am I hypnotized?" Authority figures set our expectations, condition our beliefs, and will often influence our behaviors.

How do you use this principle in your communication with your target? It's quite simple! Use certificates, social proof, testimonials, and newspaper clippings to position yourself as the obvious expert in your industry. Imagine walking into a doctor's office, and seeing a wall lined with degrees and certificates, you immediately establish more trust in that doctor because their degrees and certificates are usually an indication of their credentials. That is also why referrals work. Think about it. Someone who you trust is giving you a referral, and that creates an expectation that the professional you will hire will do a good job. It's the same if your friends set you up with someone to go on a date. They may say, "Oh you'll love this person!" That sets up an expectation based on the credibility of your friends.

4. <u>Age Is a Factor for Belief and Learning</u>

Remember how when we were children, we just believed what we were told? It's not that younger children do not have a critical factor, but it's still being formed, therefore, it is very easily bypassed. It's hard to say specifically at what age our critical factors become stronger, as it's unique to every individual. However, children are always in a state of learning, so what is presented to them is usually not analyzed on a deep level.

Think of the programs we have acquired in childhood. Some are good and some are bad. Many people carry around childhood traumas for the rest of their lives and wonder why they have a hard time letting go of those traumas. Now you know; it's due to the bypass of the critical factor and those programs become a natural part of who we are and how we respond.

You might be wondering, "Great, but my targets aren't children!" That's ok, but we can still create that childlike learning state in adults. Here's how. Assuming someone had a positive childhood, you can evoke a childlike emotion that could easily evoke a positive childlike experience and relate it to your product, service or request. One example is this, "most of my clients report that when they use our product or service (inserts your product or service here), they feel like a kid on Christmas again… Remember when you were little and that excitement you got from opening a gift on a birthday or holiday? Well, that's how most people describe our services, it's like they are just as excited as they were when they opened a gift on their 10th birthday!" By doing this, you are creating a childlike emotion and feeling state, and you are transferring that positive emotion to you, your product, or service.

5. <u>Conventional Hypnosis Versus Hypnotic Communication</u>

With conventional hypnotism, you're putting somebody into a trancelike state. They are a willing participant, and we use that trancelike state to change a behavior, feeling, emotion or habit. We evoke this trancelike state by applying a hypnotic induction. The hypnotic induction bypasses the conscious mind and allows the hypnotic suggestions to be accepted as if they were real.

Hypnotic communication does not require a hypnotic induction. It also does not require a person to be willing nor does the person have to be aware that they are being "hypnotized." It can still have very similar effects to putting somebody through an actual hypnotic process.

That brings up the ethical and moral obligations and issues again. However, please know that it is very complicated and near impossible to get a person to do something that they would not be willing to do. However, think of a family member for whom you would do anything or another person with whom you have a meaningful connection. What lengths would you go to for that person? These connections and techniques can have a very similar effect.

Some people might think, "I can't be hypnotized." But this is a state we go into every day several times a day. Anytime you daydream or zone out; you go into a more receptive state. And that's all hypnotism is. It's a type of zone, a responsive state that bypasses the conscious mind. Any information that is given to the person is not analyzed, it just goes naturally and directly into their subconscious mind. Think of a person engrossed in their cell phone, maybe on Facebook or texting. They are so consumed in that world, that they become oblivious to the outside world. While their mind is focused on their cell phone, Facebook, or text message, that is their conscious mind that is preoccupied with activity while their subconscious mind is open. While a person's subconscious mind is open, they become very receptive and suggestible. That is an excellent time to put something into their mind without them critically analyzing it. Therefore, this naturally evoking trance state will cause a person to be very receptive to outside suggestions. That can produce a very similar effect to going through a hypnotic process with a formalized hypnotic induction that causes a person to go into a receptive trance.

UNDERSTANDING NLP

When developing a hypnotic connection with someone, it is also necessary to have a general understanding of Neuro-Linguistic Programming. NLP is a way of influencing the cognitive behavior of a group or individual by using language patterns and subconscious communication skills. Think of NLP as hypnosis without hypnosis, a conversational or waking hypnosis.

Richard Bandler and John Grinder co-founded NLP in the 1970s. They studied human behavior and quick and effective ways to get people to change their internal patterns. They looked at the human mind like a programmable computer. The theory is that if you can reprogram and update a computer, we can look at the mind and human behavior in the same way. We can upgrade a person's belief systems and behaviors in the same way we update a computer's operating system to work more efficiently. Imagine trying to run a computer program from today on a Windows 95 operating system. It just wouldn't be possible. However, that's how many people are living their lives, with outdated programs and perspectives.

We all have our own map of the world, and NLP helps us connect with and work within our target's map of their reality. When we understand their reality, we can change it by reframing their perception of reality. However, before we change their programming, we first must meet them at their level.

NLP is also used to help with deeply rooted problems holding people back. It is used to cure fears, phobias, and lifelong anxieties. It has also helped people with severe clinical depression, schizophrenia, and other mental issues. NLP is also famous for helping people change habits and behaviors and also for helping athletes and others who need more of a winning mental attitude such as people in business and sales.

Chapter 4: Hypnotic Tactics

There are many variations on these types of tactics, but they offer an insight into the main things to be wary of. Examples of how each tactic can be used will be provided wherever possible to give a clear insight into how hypnotists operate in our midst, undetected, every day.

HYPNOTIC STRATEGIES

One of the best ways that you will be able to become a master of hypnosis is to experience it yourself. One method you can do to help improve your hypnotic tactics is to record yourself doing hypnosis and listen to it. If you can fully hypnotize yourself, then you can be assured you will have the skills to do this to others as well. Start by listening to other recordings of hypnosis and determine which methods have managed to work best on you.

After this, you can write your own original script. Remember; never hypnotize someone who doesn't consent to it. Hypnosis will help the other person find a state of relaxation, while also helping to persuade them to do something that is healthy or beneficial.

Like NLP, all of these methods take practice to master. Don't be discouraged because you aren't able to fully hypnotize someone else the first time you try. Take note of each hypnosis session that you have, as well. What about it worked once that didn't work as well the next time?

Remember to not use information gained from another in a hypnotic state against them either. Sometimes, they might fall into such a stupor that they become in a dreamlike state. They might say something they don't fully mean, much like a person on pain medication after getting their wisdom teeth removed might.

In contrast to manipulation, these skills are intended to be used for good purposes, as well. You might find it becomes easy to hypnotize others once you have practiced, but your motivation shouldn't be primarily for your own gain. There are benefits that both you and the entranced can gain from your hard-earned skill. However, you choose to use these powerful methods, along with the NLP tips, you can be helpful and empowering to both you and the person whom you can influence.

Understand that when you agree to hypnotize someone else, you are also given a certain responsibility. They are trusting you with a vulnerable headspace that they probably would not entrust to just anyone. Once you attempt to persuade someone, you agree to accept any negative outcomes that might happen as a result of your influence.

Healthy and positive influence will take time to build, and that is true even when you are using these hypnotic techniques. To have long-lasting persuasion that will benefit all parties is a great privilege, and it is up to you to find a positive way to utilize this power.

Anchoring

Anchoring is an NLP technique that involves linking an emotional state to some form of external stimulus. If you are familiar with the idea of Pavlovian conditioning, then you will understand this tactic. Hypnotists can induce a powerful emotion in a victim and then link it to a stimulus such as a physical gesture or tone of voice. The hypnotist is then able to induce this emotional state at will by performing the linked stimulus.

The most nefarious hypnotists will use the principle of anchoring in a very subtle and underhand way. They will work for a prolonged period of time to induce a variety of different anchors in the psyche of their victim without the victim's conscious awareness of what is taking place. This provides the manipulator with a set of hypnotic puppet strings that they can pull as and when they desire. Often, hypnotists will use an "anchor stack" to induce different intense feelings in quick succession. For example, they will induce the feeling of love, followed by terror, followed by love once more, all in quick succession. These emotions overload the victim's emotional circuitry and leaves them as mere clay in the hands of their controller.

Future Pacing

Future pacing is the closest thing possible to psychologically manipulative time travel. Future pacing allows a skilled manipulator to lead their victim on a mental journey into the future and influence behaviors and responses that will occur in the actual, chronological future that exists independent of the victim's reality.

At its most fundamental, future pacing involves the mental leading of a victim through a future scenario. For example, if the hypnotist wants their victim to feel generous and relaxed whenever they receive money, the hypnotist would ask their victim to envision a situation, such as receiving their next paycheck. To make this future imagining possible the hypnotist would ensure the victim imagined all of their five senses in action—what they would see, feel, touch etc. at the time. This helps the brain to perceive the future scenario as "real" due to its sensory depth.

Once the hypnotist cognitively transports their victim into the future, they begin to suggest certain happenings and monitor the responses. For example, the hypnotist may say something like "Imagine being very generous with this paycheck and providing it to those who really need it, because you are a kind person and doing the right thing is deep in your nature." If the victim's physical response to this future scenario showed signs of compliance and acceptance then the hypnotic manipulator would have the confidence that their victim would actually behave in this way when the scenario occurs in the future.

Due to the intensity and power of the hypnotic techniques mentioned in this chapter, the best manipulators only use them in moderation. For example, a darkly psychological hypnotist would be sure to keep their interaction with a victim 95% normal. This will increase the victim's comfort and trust to such high levels that the 5% time spent on hypnotic influence would not only slip past a victim's defenses unnoticed but would work to great effect once embedded in the victim's mind.

Future pacing is the process of taking a person into the future to see what things can be so that they can better feel the success that they can achieve. This can be used in direct hypnosis to help them completely adapt to the new feeling, belief, or habit. Everyone has an idea of what their future could be like if they made some changes in their life, alter a negative behavior, or alter a negative belief, and lived their life with these new beliefs or habits. Yes, people have these ideas clear in their minds. And future pacing lets them live it, imagine it, and thus intensify their desire for change. It allows them also to make sure that these are the changes that will benefit them. If they are not excited at the new reality, then suddenly their hypnotic processing won't actually work with them. Your correlations and causations will need to change if they are not excited about the process and about the ideas that they are working to.

When it comes to creating a permanent change in people or getting someone to take action and feel excited about taking action, future pacing is one of the major keys that will get you to that point. When you can make someone see the future, excited about the future, then you can create the path for them to get there. More than anything, combined with hypnotic logic, this produces change constantly and effectively.

Be Powerful

You can create a hypnotic state for people by simply exerting power over others. Look at how people are likely to blindly follow a person who appears to be powerful. When you do this, you can get a following and the people following you will do what you say because they want to please you and stay in your presence.

You can use this technique among your friends, family and coworkers or any person that you have a pre-existing relationship with. You want to exert your power over time so that it does not feel too aggressive. Once you notice you have followers, start small with what you are asking. They will do it without even thinking twice about it. Over time, you can ask for larger things and you will have no trouble getting them.

Mirroring

Now, the powerful approach works for people you know, but what about strangers? This is where mirroring comes into play. This allows you to quickly develop a rapport with someone once they see you both have someone in common. This can almost put them into a trance because they will naturally like you and want to please you since they will perceive both of you as very similar.

To successfully use this technique, pay attention to the stranger's common phrases and body language. Look at their behaviors. Exhibit these things back at them. As you continue your interaction with them, it will not take long for them to notice the similarities. You do not even have to lie about things you have in common.

Use Stories

The right stories can put people into a trance-like state. Think back to when you were a kid and your parents would read you stories before bed. This would induce a deep state of relaxation. The same is true when you are an adult.

As you are talking to people each day, add in some anecdotes. This shows you on a more personal level and can even give you a sense of power and authority. You want people to be able to visualize what you are saying, so use imagery when you are telling your story.

For example, you want a person to move something breakable for you because you just do not want to take the risk. Do not just ask them to move it carefully. State that you do not want the vase to be dropped since it can shatter. They will visualize the vase shattering, forcing them to not only be careful when moving it, but they will volunteer to do it. They will almost see completing the task successfully as a type of personal challenge.

Lengthy Speeches

When you want to induce hypnosis on a large group, lengthy speeches are the way to do it. Think about the television evangelists you have seen. They essentially use this form of hypnosis to get people to hand over thousands of dollars every time they hold a service.

When they are delivering their speech, they take few pauses. They use varied voice tones to annunciate points and keep people completely engrossed in what they are saying. They know what their message is, and they repeat it frequently. They often do it using different phrasing, however, so no one in the audience ever feels like something is being forced on them.

It is not uncommon for them to tell you exactly what to do without directly telling you to do it. When you are in this type of situation, you are so enamored with the speaker, that you will do just about anything they ask. They always present their lengthy speech and then they just pass the collection basket. They do not ask you to donate because they know you will because you feel dedicated to them.

This is a technique that you can use too. You do not need an auditorium for it either. If you need something from a person or a group of people, plan out a speech. Make sure that those you are talking to feel empowered throughout the speech. By the time you get to the end, you have already subconsciously implanted in their minds what you want. You will not need to ask for it. You will just get it.

For example, you want people to invest in your new business idea. Give them a speech about the business, about how much starting it would mean to you and then insert a bit of a sob story about how this is your dream, but financially, you cannot swing it. After listening to your dramatic speech, they will feel compelled to invest.

Stacking

This is a hypnotic technique that works because you essentially overwhelm the people you are talking to. With this technique, you essentially bombard people with information. They are learning so many new things that they do not have time to sort through it. They do not feel they need to check facts because you are speaking with such authority that they automatically believe what you are saying. By the time you end your thoughts, you have essentially put them into a trance.

They are completely overwhelmed and defenseless at this point. So you can tell them anything now and they will believe it. This is when you step in and use their trance-like state to your advantage. You do not directly ask for something. At this point, you just need to make a mere suggestion and you will get what you want.

Eye Cues

You can look into a person's eyes and be able to tell if someone is essentially under your spell.. When you are seeking to hypnotize, look at where their eyes are. If they are directly focused on you, you know that you have their undivided attention and you can start implanting ideas and suggestions into the subconscious.

Cold Reading

This is something that psychics use to convince people that they can actually read their mind and predict their future. You will start by making a vague statement. For example, if you know a person to be shy, you will state this. You know it is true and they will elaborate, giving you further information. You will use this further information to essentially make other predictions. Once a person feels that you have this almost clairvoyant ability, they are more prone to believe anything that you tell them.

Hypnotic Voice

First, let us focus on your hypnotic voice. Every hypnotist has a different hypnotic voice, one that is their own, one that fits their personality and that allows them to flow with their language and their suggestions to take a person on a journey. However, there are a few rules to understand the hypnotic process and the building of one's hypnotic voice.

First and foremost, it is understood that your tone is everything and it must be consistent.

A person will accept just about any form of hypnotic voice, as long as the process is consistent. It does not have to be relaxing. It does not have to be soft and gentle. It has to be consistent. Now, what does that mean?

A consistent voice is one that maintains whatever tone it has set up for. Whether it is dynamic or monotone, whether it is soft or average level, people go into trance with ease once they hear what you have to say. Anything that distracts them, including your voice, will hinder their ability to enter hypnosis and can break and interrupt the trance once they are in it. A consistent tone avoids that, allowing their brain to focus on what you are saying rather than on how you are saying it.

Second, you should always establish a flow with your voice. Flow is simply the process of moving from one topic to the next with a good transition. That'll come with practice, but, the easiest way to think about it, is having a few simple phrases that take people from one place to the next in their mind, creating bridges to deeper and deeper hypnotic processes. The flow of the voice makes it even more hypnotic and more powerful than most anything else you will do in hypnosis. It takes a person deep into the trance and comfortable with going deeper and deeper into their hypnotic process.

But you might be wondering what type of hypnotic voice you can develop, and what the hypnotic voice should be?

For the longest time, and still, in some hypnotic schools, you will hear that hypnosis is supposed to be done in a slow, monotone voice that pretty much bores a person into relaxation and trance. This method was formed from some of the early schools of hypnosis as the clearest way of taking anyone and giving them the ability to hypnotize someone. Anyone can talk really slow, announce each word, and take their time when talking.

This method does work. Some great hypnotists have used that method throughout the years to great results for their clients. The problem with this method is that for some people it is just a turnoff and there will always be some people that just cannot respond to it. It is not how their mind works. As NLP teaches when it comes to mirroring and matching, the best forms of rapport building come from matching their voice and their tone including the speed of their voice. When you are using a monotone voice, you will face people for whom that voice just does not work on.

That is where the dynamic vocal approach can be very effective, and one of the best options if you can learn how to master it. It does require a greater amount of effort and it is something that does take some skill but not a huge amount to really get good at. It requires you to be able to do two things. One, using fluctuation in your voice, where you emphasize and deemphasize things all with the tone of your voice while keeping it flowing, consistent, and clear. Another thing that has to be done is to match their tone. If they are a fast talker, you want to pick up your pace when you are initially taking them into a trance, and if they are a slow talker, you want to slow yourself down more.

Every important point draws them in first with a lowering of the voice, as they then pick up their voice to make sure that as they have drawn you in, and you are now listening to their every word. This can be repeated in hypnosis and especially on their unconscious mind, making each command more powerful, and making them quicker and more reliably going into trance.

Of course, in the end, you are the person that will be using the hypnosis and using these skills, so it is up to you how you do them and what you do. It is also about what you are comfortable with and how well you can do what you are comfortable with. That is a major importance. It is all about you. A hypnotist must discover their own style as if they must discover their own inductions that they like to use. You can make adjustments for clients, but, in general, when you are working with hypnosis it is all about what makes you feel the best.

Hypnotic Logic

The more you relax, the better you feel. Hypnotic logic is correlation and causation because that is how our brains work. Whether correlation and causation are real, we ourselves look for these things when it comes to every area of our lives. It is such a common practice that we have to remember to exclude this type of reasoning when we are doing actual research. But, when it comes to a person and their life, creating these correlative and causative thoughts is the power that hypnosis has to makes your suggestions powerful and transforms the person's mind. As you will learn when we talk about Direct Suggestions next, when you give suggestions to people, you have to do so in a way that their mind will accept, see the reason in, and be able to actually adapt to themselves.

Hypnotic logic, as you will learn in the next chapter, on advanced hypnosis, where we will talk about indirect hypnosis, can be used at every solitary phase of hypnosis, and in fact, it needs to be. From the induction phase to the hypnotic suggestions to the post-talk, at every point, you want to establish the experiences they will face and using those potential experiences, explain how they will correlate with their hypnotic suggestions.

Correlation is at first the most important thing to understand about the hypnotic logic, with much of the hypnotic language using correlative terms, or comparative terms, to help form for people the new behavior or new beliefs that someone wants to install. Things like, "the moment you want to go for a cigarette is the moment you remember your desire to be healthy," creating for their mind a correlation to their health and their desire to stop cigarettes. The more you relax the better you feel, as you think about your amazing life that you will have, you become more and more comfortable with making these changes.

Direct Suggestions

A direct suggestion has the issue that people's minds will occasionally try to reject an outside command. Let us face it we are by and large a stubborn people and our brains are always trying to maintain the status quo (even if the status quo is trying to kill us). Your brain, a client's brain, the human brain as it is creating every habit and every belief as a way to help a person through their problems and through their life. This is very important to understand because it understands that to the brain that you are trying to convince, you are going against what they feel is necessary for their survival. So more important than anything, every suggestion should be based around their wants and their statements.

This is also why using future pacing and hypnotic logic is incredibly important when putting together your direct suggestions. The more you can make the suggestions feel exciting and the more you can make the mind ready to accept it, the easier these direct suggestions will be taken in. With that, there is one other thing to do to make direct suggestions even more powerful.

Positive and Affirmative Language

The mind rarely hears the word cannot, will not, do not, no… negative terms get negative results. This is one of the major things that the Law of Attraction has gotten right. Being positive and creating a positive reality, rather than trying to use the negative stimulus to get them to fall in line and respond. There are some points where giving a negative suggestion can hold weight and be used. From quitting smoking to no longer feel anxious, and other such direct suggestions. But, for every bit of negativity, you want more and more positivity to go along with it.

This is why you want to make sure that you always lean to the positive and affirmative with your suggestions, thus promoting an exciting and positive outlook at every end. Some old school hypnosis used to have people look at their pain. They would imagine what would happen to them if they did not give up their habits, and though this has its place in a more detailed and more powerful structure when you are doing basic hypnosis, it is easier and faster just to stick to the positive.

HOW TO HYPNOTIZE PEOPLE

Talking about any professional hypnosis instructor, they tend to notify their clients that a successful hypnotherapist person is usually a confidential person. Ideally, you motivate confidence in your clients with the method of "personality assurance." In other words, the clients get to the state, whereby they feel better when you are around. Of course, this is the same when you invent the method of delivering speeches to hypnotize your audience. To start with, you need to cultivate confidence in your ability when with the audience, and you portray a nervous mood at the same time.

Ideally, you tend to put your client/audience in the state of which they feel like you cannot find them in the room; you portray the narratives in their minds. This could be done with the ideology of focusing your attention so carefully to ensure that your words have a real effect on their perception, consciously and unconsciously. Changing the functioning of your immune system or blood circulation tends to be done by a competent hypnotist.

A good narrator must understand the idea of you wanting to be sufficiently convincing your listeners to concentrate on what you say. This is necessary because you need them to disassociate themselves from their concerns and situations to travel to different times, places, and opportunities with you. So, at least for a while, you tend to make them understand the benefits of implementing the new ways of seeing reality.

Helping people learn new ways of responding to life with the aim of not letting low confidence, phobias, and attention mess them up is so useful when it comes to "therapy hypnosis. You concentrate the attention of your audience so selectively when you speak powerfully, that they become hypnotic rather than pure awareness of the essence of their living. Therefore, this kind of education seems more profound for people.

Avoiding the Boredom Trance

However, it appears that various kinds of trances are in the crowd. You tend to hypnotize the audience by making them be in the state of leaving the room psychologically when you aren't inspiring. Instead, the groups will try not to obey your concept but try to avoid your voice. In most cases, they will begin imagining what they will do for the day, what their next social arrangements will be like, or even what they will cook for lunch. The audience/participant tends to be disassociating, but not the ways we would like. However, it appears that the specific technique to guide your audience to the proper direction seems to be available.

Crowd hypnosis

Professional public presenters tend to captivate the audience with thoughts and words. Also, what they will use are the anticipation, vocabulary, narrative, and initial pace. This means that implementing the ideas for their audience to act on in the future will be their ideal objective. This method tends to be very useful when it comes to hypnotizing the audience. This means that the hypnotic speakers don't give just facts. Instead, they serve the audience with an experience that will improve the way they feel, think, or even behave.

Ideally, hypnotic performance tends to take part in referring the brain to the most meaningful pieces of music and poetry. Public talks that are effective have a real rhythm. The kind of trance rhythm that draws you in when it comes to the best speeches, such as the best hypnotic inductions.

According to Sir Winston Churchill

The usage of persuasive expression through repetition was Sir Winston Churchill's idea. He portrays an impression of having a positive future that's beyond the present difficult times. Also, he doesn't lie to his listeners, so he pretends that things are straightforward. Besides, Churchill brings up sharp images that are important to his audience. He focuses on escaping an approaching Dark Age through intense, proud, courageous, and then mutual struggle just as the storytelling language or even epic mythology. Churchill's dialect tends to be misleading, which is his favorite hypnotic strategy. And this was actually explained in some of his speeches.

A speaker may choose to implement the use of deliberate confusion. And then appeal to the unconscious to bind the conscious mind. In most cases, the meaning untangles before the psyche comes to conscious awareness. For example, so many tend to have not owed so much. For instance, you do this when you want to be more hypnotic, to captivate their attention and hypnotize them.

Prepare your speech with words that appeal feelings

"Nominalizations" happens to be the term in which the people who have to travel inward to communicate with personal meanings are called. This idea helps in hypnotizing the audience. These happen to be words like; mighty, lovely, devotion, wisdom, power, and so on. What's just needed is that you ensure that you align the terms with what you mean. Ideally, such correctly used terms need to contain more than mere words of the form of concrete.

Paint Vision of hearing minds through combining senses

We portray a paradise-like experience to someone, the moment we hypnotize them. And indeed, in pictures, words, sounds, feelings, tastes, and as well as emotions, we dream. You need to tell what you've seen, felt, heard, and tasted when you say to a story about something that has happened to you when giving speeches. Ideally, an address becomes more elegant with the implementations of this sensory appeal. For instance, "When I heard a sickening scream, I was carrying a huge bag through the mall, I turned around and saw two giant guys trying to mug an old lady who pushed them" sounds more appropriate. Compared to this, "I went to the shopping center and witnessed a serious physical conflict."

Fascinate with your voice

Think about words that have significance and relevance. So, in other words, you need to speed up with your voice at times. Then sometimes slow down a bit. Perhaps, this shouldn't be every time to avoid getting your audience upset. Then you need to reduce the speed you implement in your words when you make an argument of significance. Then, in addition, you can even talk to a real hypnotist calmly and in slow delivery periodically.

Use Suddenness

We tend to go into a hypnotic spell when we're shocked or surprised, not only when we loosen up. Humor, as it is, tends to amuse someone. So, great speakers implement the idea of using humor because it is hypnotic. In some other perspectives, there tends to be a punch on a punch line, and that is because it is surprising. Mainly, the shock is often used by the hypnotists from the different stages to track subjects quickly into a hypnotic state.

Hypnotic Inductions

This happens to be the mechanism a hypnotist utilizes to put the patient in a state whereby they are more open to suggestions. Ideally, the hypnotic induction happens to be the first stage in hypnosis.

There are various types of inductions which are:

Relaxation technique: Why do the therapists put people on a cushy leather couch and then ask you to make yourself comfortable? This is more than mere courtesy. Relaxation is a tool that hypnotists use, and this happens to be a standard method for psychologists.

The clients fall into a trance when they are relaxed, and the minds appear to be willing to try something new. They are more likely to speak with the instructor and at the same time, be open to indirect suggestions.

Here are a few relaxation techniques:

- Calm yourself down
- Rest
- Start a rundown in your mind
- Be mindful of your breathing
- Make sure your muscles are calm
- Say your words softly

Handshake technique: Milton Erickson implemented the usage of the handshake technique as a method to induce a hypnotic trance. Ideally, a handshake is well known to be our society's most common form of greetings.

The handshake happens to be a shock on the unconscious because the idea violates the common social practice.

The hypnotist disrupts the pattern our mind has developed with the method of holding the wrist and dragging the person involved forward and off-balance instead of going through the society's general idea of shaking hands frequently. The subconscious mind is unexpectedly open to the suggestions that are being portrayed when the pattern is disrupted.

Eyes cues: The subconscious handles the left side of the two brain spheres while the right tolerates the creative, practical, and conscious side. To see how the listeners, respond to the hypnotist utterances, they look for feedbacks from them in any conversation. Then the instructor looks at the eyes of the person involved. To know if they are looking at the right, to the conscious or unconscious or even to the left, or if they are fixed in the room on an element. Then the hypnotist makes a suggestion when they enter the dormant state that they are consciously not aware of.

Incentive eye contact: A typical case of use is the reading of the eye movement. This is a common usage; yet, the hypnotist knows that hypnotic induction can also be done on the listener. Ideally, as the speaker, you can also perform a hypnotic induction on the listener with the help of the eye movement. Stephen Brooks developed and tested this new technique.

Visualization: For trance making and suggestion making, this is also a method that can be implemented. For instance, ask your listener to picture every detail in a room they can remember and that which they are familiar with, the floor, the window design, the wall paintings, the smell, and the light. Then change to a stay with which they are less familiar. At the point when they battle to recollect the careful restraints, they open their brains to suggestions. Besides, Use perception to recall and liken positive recollections with a compensating activity. Or try to adjust one's perspective on a negative image. Envision positive pictures, and memories like a wedding, birthday, or graduation.

Using Arm Levitation: The customer begins by shutting their eyes with this standard Ericksonian strategy. The trance inducer makes proposals about each arm's sensations. For instance, we may state that the gun feels substantial or light, hot or cold. The patient enters a stupor state and can lift their arm physically. Or cause them to accept that they have raised their arm. The usage tends to be successful in any case.

Unexpected shock/inversion: Carefully continue! Like the procedure of handshake, a stunning subject can enter a daze. I wouldn't ever propose making any agony and distress a subject. However, by stepping on a lady's foot and following her with a recommendation, Erickson once showed this. A gentler structure would be the "certainty drop" you may have known about at a group building occasion or took an interest in. The sentiment of falling back alarms the cerebrum and opens the brain to the proposal. However, one must be sure that the subject won't be lost.

Eye Fixation: Have you at any point saw that you were daydreaming while somebody is talking and taking a gander at an intriguing item in the room? Have you overlooked what they said? Possibly you've been in a daze. It is conceivable to utilize any object of the center to actuate stupor. The most well-known models are the vitality pendulum or a swinging pocket watch. Even as the two most popular things are currently synonymous with the entrancing of the hokey stage. Due to their ubiquity, you are bound to fizzle and face opposition utilizing these things.

Body scan: This is a regular self-mesmerizing technique, beginning with your eyes shut at the highest point of the body, then scan gradually from the head to the feet. Note each sensation. The breath opening the ribs, the feelings in your arm, each finger end, at that point the feet on the ground should be noted. Rescan from the bottom to top of the cycle. Keep on looking over and down until you get into the trance.

Furthermore, to expand viability, the body output can be stacked with different systems of spellbinding acceptance. For example, commencement breathing, and unwinding can be used to develop sustainability.

Commencement Breathing: You will, in general, have known about unwinding controlled relaxing. In any case, it can likewise be a straightforward type of self-spellbinding. Close your eyes as you sit straight in a seat with your legs on your lap. Preferably, that is how it works. Breathe through your nose and your eyes. Every exhalation considers an interim. You may be in a daze over the long haul. If not, check down from a higher number to proceed with the activity.

Entrancing Suggestions: A proposal is the client's ideal conduct. After an entranced individual enters the stupor, post-sleep inducing recommendations are given: a state wherein they are increasingly open to impact.

Circuitous Suggestion: Erickson was the author of Circuitous Suggestion. It is compelling because it puts the power in the subject's hands instead of those of the master, concerning the patient's limits and restorative ethics. Additionally, it has exhibited continuously convincing questions that are protected or suspicious of a daze. You should you become acquainted with Ericksonian Hypnosis.

Direct Suggestion: In conversational entrancing, a prompt proposition is an expression headed to play out a particular movement. Even though this is inconceivable; sometimes, it is observed as exploitative because, as the leader of the position, you are intended to control the client. The client doesn't control the decision to change lead with this strategy. The Stanford Prison Experiment was an unbelievable instance of using authority, passive consent, and direct recommendations to control subjects. Here are some model suggestions: "you will rest," "you will stop smoking," and "you will get in shape."

Voice Tone: This is especially significant when making a suggestion. This can be combined with various techniques like loosening up. Also, you may wish to get free in the above model; the word free is verbally expressed gently and drawn out. You can make a quick proposition, "you will STOP smoking"! Another perfect pair for voice tone is the confusion system. The master could move the way of talking from mumbling to shouting. Converse with a substitute feature, or use a drawl, to bewilder the subject.

Sleep inducing trigger: You will be amazed to realize that there are such vast numbers of trancelike triggers. This trigger causes the subliminal to recall a perfect action or feeling which was proposed under the spell. Here are a few sleep-inducing triggers; Opening eyes, the sound of a chime, a snap of fingers, clapping, standing up or sitting down.

Don't be surprised about this: what makes google riddles behind the obsession of the ear. Initially, the item keeps the cognizant personality caught up with the opening to the recommendation of the intuitive.

Chapter 5: Using Emotion to Create Hypnotic Connection

Heightened emotional states are really useful when influencing, persuading, and connecting with people. Imagine what it would be like to strike up any emotion you want in a person. Think about the potential you would have to influence them.

You can easily convey a positive or negative emotion in your target and connect that emotion to any place or anything you want. I know some business owners who use this unethically.

They will evoke a very negative emotion in their customer or prospect and connect that negative emotion to their competition. The same goes for love interests. I have seen people manipulate a love interest to feel a very negative emotion and connect that emotion to their current partner, and then evoke a positive emotion and get their love interest to connect that to them. You can only imagine the moral and ethical problems with this. But remember, if people are manipulated into doing something they do not want to do, it will come back to bite the manipulator in the butt.

Manipulating or coercing a person to do something they do not want to do or buy something they do not want to buy differs from persuading. Persuading is helping influence a person's behavior or decision, to make that decision easier. Often, people will buy something on a whim or because they feel a certain emotion even though they do not need or want what they bought. Later, when they get home, they will often realize or at least stop and think, "Wait, I really didn't want nor need that. Why did I buy that? I am going to return this!" What results is buyer's remorse, and the victim will often regret their decision, feel taken advantage of, and resent the person they felt took advantage.

Remember, emotions are one way that bypasses the critical mind. When a person experiences a heightened state of emotion, their subconscious mind is more open and receptive, and whatever happens around or connected to that emotional state will often create a behavior or a response in the target's subconscious mind. You can do this by evoking a positive emotion or a negative emotion and connect or relate those emotions to something to get your target to think, feel or respond in a way you want them to. One of the positive ways to lower barriers is by using laughter. When people are laughing and having fun, they rarely have their guard up, it's lowered and they are easier to influence because they are not expecting to be sold or swayed or even learn. There are several hypnotic emotion evoking words that will cause a person to go to a time where they felt a certain way or create a time where they would feel that way. These emotions we evoke in people are called "arousal emotions." It's not like it sounds. These are emotions that keep your target alert and interested in wherever you direct their attention. These emotions should be substantial enough to get a reaction out of people, and the emotional buzz words will help with that.

The first step, before you evoke emotion with one of the emotional buzzwords is to identify how you want them to feel, or how they should feel. What do you want them to feel? What should they feel? Why should they feel that way? Now let's get into the emotional hypnotic buzzwords that can help evoke these emotions.

EMOTIONAL HYPNOTIC BUZZWORDS

Imagine, picture, visualize, think about, think about a time when...

These are words and phrases that evoke emotions and feelings in the subconscious mind. Remember, when you evoke emotion, you are getting to the subconscious mind which will allow your target to see themselves feeling good about deciding. You can use any combination of these words, in fact, mix it up a little! You will want to mix it up because everyone communicates a bit differently. Some people will report they can think about something, but they have a hard time imagining it. Others will say they can picture something, but not visualize, and all other combinations.

Let's look at a few examples of how this can work.

Let's first work with evoking positive emotions. Let's pick an example of asking someone to go on a date. "Think about how much fun we will have when we go to the baseball game; it will be just like the time we saw each other at Jamie's party and laughed so hard we were spitting out our drinks! Remember that? I don't even remember what we were talking about, do you? So, when should I pick you up so we can go to the game?" You want to move them through the emotional ladder to get them in a more positive state. When we feel better about something, we will be more likely to agree and say yes!

That can also be helpful in a sales situation. Let's say you are trying to sell someone a computer. Before you use any of the emotional buzzwords, you first want to find out their motivation for buying the computer. Let's say they need a computer that is faster and has more memory. They are sick and tired of waiting 5 minutes to open a program, and they hate having to carry around an external hard drive. Knowing this, you may say, "Imagine taking the computer home and being able to use it right out of the box. Say goodbye to all of those old issues. Think about how much faster you'll be getting things done on your new laptop, and you can look forward to keeping everything contained so that you can leave that old external hard drive behind!"

ANCHORING POSITIVE EMOTIONS

You may have already caught onto this, but you can anchor a positive emotion, or a negative emotion just as easy as it is to evoke that emotion.

Once you evoke that emotion, you then have the target picture themselves feeling that emotion about you, your product, or service. In the baseball game example, we had the target go back into their memory and think of a time where they felt good. After accessing that feeling, it was then connected to the baseball game — so, they saw themselves feeling the same positive way in the future situation.

You can do this with negative emotions as well. Evoke them and attach them to something. Without getting too political, you see this happening with a lot of political figures. When you look at a commercial around election time, it starts off with evoking a negative emotion by showing some horrible images, such as little children starving, people dying in a hospital bed, or some other very gut-wrenching image. Then it says something like, "This is what will happen if you elect (insert candidate here)."

THE STRENGTH OF EXCITING EMOTIONS AND LOVE

Once we increase the feelings of confidence, reduce the feelings of anxiety, and establish an unstoppable state of mind, people often ask me "What is the ideal first date?"

A lot of studies have been done on what to do and where to go. Believe it or not, studies have shown that going to the movies is the worst first date you could go on. A good first date should start off with something that elevates levels of excitement and something that gets endorphins flowing. When we start that flow of endorphins, we feel good, and the level of oxytocin and dopamine (the chemicals responsible for love and happiness) also flow, and we connect those feelings to the person. If you will incorporate a dinner into the date, it's best to do the invigorating part of the date first, and then go to dinner afterward, because then you can talk about those positive experiences.

Chapter 6: Setting Boundaries for Yourself and Others

Being able to set boundaries for yourself, either as a subject or a hypnotist, is such an important part of hypnosis as a culture, which so often becomes overlooked because many people take it for granted. We treat boundaries strangely, in that many people imagine boundaries as static, things that don't ever change and which remain a defining factor a person. However, anyone you ever meet will likely have boundaries which change from session to session, from subject to subject. The boundaries we set for ourselves and the boundaries other people set for themselves almost always change, and are always something that needs to be asked about before every single session.

No matter how well you know the person you're working with, asking them about their boundaries and limits not only lets them know that you care about their comfort, but it also gives you an idea of where to take the induction. If a subject tells you that they have a bit of a problem with really harsh wording when it comes to hypnosis—they don't know why for sure, they just know that it makes them uncomfortable to be spoken to too professionally by a hypnotist—you, as their hypnotist, now know much more specifically how to phrase parts of your script to cater more toward that specific person and their preferences as a subject. Because you asked about their preferences and boundaries, you avoided what would've made that subject uncomfortable, even though you had only the best intentions as their hypnotist. As we communicate better with one another, we also learn how to best navigate through situations based on the other person, what we think they're probably going to say.

Assuming is a fine thing to do with a person you know well when the situation doesn't involve hypnosis—although recreational hypnosis is in no way exclusively romantic, it is something very intimate, simply because it allows the hypnotist almost free reign of the mind of their subject. Because hypnosis is so intimate, many people may feel violated if their hypnotist goes ahead and conducts themselves how they see fit without first consulting their subject, and accidentally hits a nerve during the session. It's that intimacy that's so often paired with extreme trust, which may have been violated since the hypnotist took for granted the boundaries of their subject.

A hypnotist can have pure and only good intentions at heart for their partner but by violating that trust and accidentally overstepping a boundary they didn't know existed can be the cause of a strained relationship between a hypnotist and their partner. Even if the hypnotist does ask about their subject's boundaries, not being careful to adhere strictly to them can cause problems between them and their subject. It can be hard to keep that note always in your head, though, and mistakes are made. If a subject is unwilling to forgive a single mistake that a hypnotist made in good but forgetful faith, that pair may not be suited well to each other. Keeping in mind the boundaries of your subject, even as a beginning hypnotist, likely puts you ahead of some of your peers who are also starting out as novice hypnotists. Taking the time to try and care for and cater to your hypnotist—while, of course, still minding your own boundaries and limitations—automatically sets you apart from at least some of your "competition".

Showing your subject that you care for their comfort and well-being, even just as a hypnotist and not as a friend, can genuinely go a long way with your subject, depending on their personality and how they respond to different levels of affection. In the sense of feeling comfortable, a big way to help someone to feel comfortable is to make them feel safe. It's so incredibly important to listen and make your subject feel listened to and cared for, as you often don't know how much stress that subject is under. It can be hard to be constantly on the ball and listening to everything the subject has to say to you, but simply making them feel seen and acknowledged can go particularly far in making sure they understand that you're more and willing to listen to and adhere to their boundaries, no matter what they may be.

Of course, knowing a subject's boundaries and adhering to them throughout the entirety of the session are two very different things. Even if you register that a subject has a specific sensation or aesthetic or sensation that they want to avoid at all costs, you still have to utilize that information and be able to substitute anything in your script that may have collided with that boundary with something more suitable to that specific person. This can be hard, especially if you're the kind of hypnotist who exclusively writes their scripts beforehand and isn't used to making any kind of change right before the session begins.

However, the ability to quickly creatively substitute those details out, as well as going that extra mile to take care of your subject and make them know that you've listened to them and will follow up on your promise to do everything you can to make them comfortable, also puts you considerably ahead of others who are beginning as hypnotists. Not to mention, your subject will also highly appreciate that gesture of kindness and compassion. If your subject hasn't outwardly told you before a session what their limits or preferences are, it's acceptable to simply ask them. Even if it sounds too blunt, it's much better to embarrass yourself for a moment then to purposefully avoid the question and later find out that you made your subject upset without even intending to.

If your subject has boundaries that they've thought of, they should tell you when prompted. If, however, your subject doesn't have any specific boundaries that come to mind, allow them to think about it for a minute. If they can't think of anything, it's fine to proceed how you would have normally with the induction. However, along the way, periodically check in with your subject in a trance to make sure they're still comfortable. When going about this, make sure your prompting isn't so blunt that it pulls the subject directly out of the trance. If they're deeply entranced, simply slip in a "Nod your head/tell me 'yes' if you're comfortable and relaxed right now...". Whenever you notice a large chunk of time in the session has passed and are bringing the subject out of trance afterward, check in on them again to ask if they felt uncomfortable at any point during the session. The answer would ideally by "no", but if it doesn't, understand what exactly pushes the boundary for your subject and helps you better understand them and make the experience for them better if there will be a next session with them. If there will be a foreseeable next session with that person, in particular, ask them to try and think of any boundaries they might have. At the next session, when you get together, ask them if they've thought of anything. Continuing that process of thinking about your boundaries and how they've changed, if at all, helps the two of you come together and understand each other significantly better. It also helps you understand yourself much better, just taking a small chunk of time often to reflect on how you've changed and grown and whether or not any of those changes have a correlation with something that's happened recently in your life to place stress on you.

While the boundaries of the subject are certainly important, it's also very important not to neglect the boundaries and preferences of yourself, the hypnotist. Your boundaries also influence how you write up your scripts, how you behave toward your subject, and how you think of your sessions. Having an open conversation with your subject about boundaries can be a good way to not only be open about their boundaries but to be open about yours as well. If a subject you're seeing has a preference or a boundary which directly collides with your own, don't sacrifice your comfort and mental health for the comfort of the subject—although many people like to think that the more important person in a hypnotist/subject pair is the subject, the one who receives the most focus and the most instruction, the two people are evenly matched in importance.

As such, don't let the desires and preferences of the subject obscure what you personally prefer, and feel is best for yourself and your well-being. If the subject, however, directly interferes with those boundaries of yours, it's likely in your best interest and the best interest of the subject that the two of you cease seeing each other. Even if the subject is in no way directly harmful to you and has your best interests at heart the way you have their best interests at heart, it's likely that the two of you interacting in the context of a session could result in very unsavory results. Obviously, the ideal is a situation in which both the subject and the hypnotist want essentially the same thing out of each other. Of course, that happening is fairly uncommon, but it's something to be compromised on.

Whether or not you're a hypnotist with very specific preferences and boundaries, or just someone who has a vague understanding of their partner's boundaries, compromising between yourself and your subject is one of the most important aspects of hypnosis.

Because we so often take communication for granted or fear that communicating properly will take away from the atmosphere of the session, many subjects and hypnotists simply don't communicate their concerns or their issues within the session to one another. Even when in trance, many subjects don't let their hypnotists know if they have a problem or feel uncomfortable. It can be hard to try and better communications when your subject simply doesn't seem to be able to bring themselves to communicating clearly—you can never force someone to speak clearly how they feel and why, but you can offer them a stress-free and calm environment where they can share their feelings, or at least be more likely to do so. Because people in the recreational hypnosis scene so often feel as though communicating an issue to their partner takes away from the ideal image of hypnosis, in which everything falls into place perfectly, they often don't feel comfortable expressing concerns about a session to their hypnotist, especially when in the middle of trance.

Even the subconscious has a way of burying things that it doesn't want to be open about—this is where repressed memories come from. Because a lot of subjects feel much pressured to let everything fall into place on its own, many problems occur because of that miscommunication. When miscommunication happens, the relationship between the subject and their hypnotist can easily become more and more strained. When two people don't talk to each other even though they both know something isn't right, both parties get the feeling that they're being ignored. So, when in a position during a session where you feel uncomfortable for any reason, let the other person know as soon as you see fit. Whether it be right at that moment, or waiting until after the session is over, alerting your partner that something they've done affected you negatively is the only way they'll better understand you, your boundaries, and how to best take care of you as a subject or hypnotist.

There are some kinds of subjects, and some kinds of hypnotists, who naturally feel less compelled to open up to others about how they feel and why they feel that way, especially in the concept of something intimate, like hypnosis. This can be due to anything or nothing at all. Sometimes a subject will have issues at their home, with their friends or family, or some other kind of stress which puts them in an emotional position to close off. Other subjects are almost always closed off this way, possibly because of the way they were raised and possible because that's simply their personality. Even though it can be frustrating at time to have a subject who habitually doesn't open up to you, even if they have a problem, you can't get anywhere with that problem by pestering them to open up to you. It simply won't work, the more you ask and beg the subject to open up to you, the more they'll be turned off even from the idea of telling you when they have a problem that crops up, either inside a session or outside in their everyday life. While constantly pushing your subject to open up to you is usually not a very good idea, there are many ways that you, as a partner, can try and encourage them to be more open, like taking care of them whenever possible. This can work for many subjects, as they likely will instinctively want to return the treatment that you've been giving them. Even if you feel as if you're coddling them, placing them in a comforting and welcoming environment is exactly what someone who feels uncomfortable opening up needs—unless the subject openly recognizes what you're doing and asks you directly to stop.

While comforting a person often does allow them to feel more willing to be open, some people just need more space and time than others to be able to open up to those around them emotionally. Additionally, when we treat a person a certain way for an extended period of time, the other person naturally begins to reciprocate. So, after a certain amount of time spent going out of your way to care for your subject or hypnotist, that partner will soon find themselves caring for you as well, which leads to more communication. More directly, a partner is much more likely to communicate if you communicate with them often. Not so much that you may come off as obnoxious, but enough so that the partner gets the picture—communication is a massive part of how your relationships function, and you won't be sacrificing that anytime soon.

Often, we find ourselves in a place where we feel uncomfortable with something, but we aren't sure if it's a "valid" boundary to have or not. There are many things that people consider their boundaries, and which are subject to change because we grow out of those fears or sources of discomfort. Some people stick with the same boundaries their entire life. All subjects and hypnotists are different and will have different ways they face their limits/boundaries. Some subjects aren't willing to acknowledge why they have what limits they do, and don't want to be pushed to think about them, although more subjects can consider the reasons, they may have the limits that they do. All of those reactions are normal, and it's important to understand that even if you feel as though there's something off about your limits, or you actively want to change them, there are healthy and unhealthy ways to go about doing so.

Some ways that are unhealthy include:

Hiding your boundary from your partner because you think that it's subject to change – not only are your boundaries often a bit unpredictable, but there's no difference in importance between a boundary that you think is permanent and one that you think is temporary or subject to change. A temporary boundary is still on which correlates to how certain sensations make you feel—they're still a part of your comfort zone, even if that comfort zone is temporary. If you don't let your partner know what is and isn't good for you emotionally, even if only for one session, they know better how to move away from certain topics if they know that some specific content may cross one of your boundaries. It's never a good idea to hide any of your boundaries or limits from your partner within the session—ignoring your limit will only allow the cause for the boundary to grow stronger and control your life more. No matter you're the reason, it's always in your best interest as either a subject or a hypnotist, to tell the other person in the party about all the boundaries you have that could pertain to or crop up during that session. If you avoid talking about them, you're only delaying whenever a problem will show up for you.

Just "sticking it out" and "manning up" – whether you're a man or not, being able to take the emotional high road for yourself and tell your partner is anything crosses a line or makes you uncomfortable is what will encourage them to do the same if the need ever arose. Showing your subject/hypnotist that you're more than willing to open up to them gives them a great example to follow, one that will help them also take care of themselves better in the long run. The concept of simply sticking it out if something makes you uncomfortable during a session, just dealing with it, stretches what you are and aren't willing to deal with that crosses your boundary. Stretching that boundary too far can have fairly harmful results for both you and your partner. So, not only is it important to tell your partner immediately if and when something crosses a boundary of yours, but it's also very important that when you set boundaries for yourself, set them hard. Having soft boundaries, ones that don't apply in certain circumstances or can be pushed around a little if need be allowed for not only a potentially malicious partner to take advantage of that, but it allows for your own comfort to be easily compromised by even a well-intentioned partner. Because you haven't drawn a clear line in the sand just yet as to how you know you want to be treated, the subject or hypnotist can only pick and choose and guess what might work for you.

Setting harder boundaries allow for much more clarity when you work with someone else. This allows for much less miscommunication and much fewer understandings between the subject and their hypnotist. If they ask about boundaries, tell them your hard boundaries and say them firmly. Building up your sense of confidence in where you stand boundary-wise makes you more able to stand by those boundaries when the time comes. In the place of a hypnotist, being able to firmly say where your boundaries lie also makes you seem much more confident and surer of yourself, a green light for almost all subjects that you know what you're doing.

Some much healthier things to do include:

Being able to communicate clearly and frequently, maybe even a bit too much – communication is by far, the most important part of having a good relationship with your subject or hypnotist within hypnosis. Sometimes, you have to choose between shutting up and not saying anything about a concern or question you might have, and obnoxiously bringing up the same concern frequently in a string of conversation. Even if that conversation is one-sided, choose to be a bit obnoxious communicating with your partner too much means a lot more than not communicating with them enough. Being able to annoy them a little is only an added perk to the pros of letting your partner know exactly what's up and why you want something changed, and anything else you may have a concern with. If that particular partner doesn't want to hear it out of you, tries to shut you down, or otherwise makes you feel guilty for trying to rise up a concern, it might be time to leave them as a hypnotic partner. It's possible that the way you're trying to communicate with that partner is unsavory, in which case it's important to take a step back and evaluate yourself, but if your partner doesn't want to deal with someone whose only intention is to communicate, that's on them and you'd be much better off with a partner who is much keener on active communication with one another. While very few people really appreciate a partner who's constantly in their faces disrupting the flow of conversation with information about themselves when the situation doesn't call for it, it's much better to have that situation than one in which a subjects emotional safety is put at risk because they decided to keep their boundaries locked up and didn't decide to let their hypnotist know about their limits. Not only is it simply a good idea, and not only do you have a responsibility and obligation to yourself to let your partner know when someone comes up, but you also have a responsibility to your partner to tell them about your limits, what you do and don't like. Telling them as soon as possible and reminding them could be the difference between a feel-good session and one that ends in a panic attack.

Taking time to reflect on your limits and understanding them better – you don't have to keep all your trancing boundaries written down and locked up in a diary. Additionally, the reflection you have on yourself doesn't have to be everyday or every other day. It shouldn't be too often, actually, lest you get bored of it quickly however, it's always a good idea to take a moment and step back, looking at your boundaries objectively. While it obviously helps to better understand what exactly your boundaries are before you enter a new session with a potentially new subject or hypnotist, introspection can also help you better understand why you have those boundaries, where they come from, how they've changed over time, and how you can predict they'll change going forward. Having this kind of time where you can better understand yourself also allows you to more eloquently talk about boundaries with your partner. Encourage them to also take that time to sit back and think about themselves and their limits in the context of hypnosis. While not everyone can see immediate results or reach a new place of enlightenment after doing so, it still helps to clear the mind and to focus on what's important in the context of the session and your relationship with your subject or hypnotist.

Being able to focus on the best possible way to communicate with your partner opens up many ways to perfect the experiences that the two of you have with one another. Although the importance of communication and boundary is so often pushed aside, hypnosis may be considered a crime if there weren't such an emphasis on the importance of drawing a line in the sand. Taking the time you may need to consider your communication with your subject, their communication with you, and understanding how the two of you can improve and make the experience better mutually, shows that you are both responsible enough to call yourselves experiences hypnotists and subjects. Two people who can work together and make an experience better every time they repeat it—that responsibility is a trademark of both an experienced hypnotist, and a very good one.

Chapter 7: Stage Hypnosis and Covert Persuasion

Stage hypnosis is what most of our preconceived notions of hypnosis is – a dimly lit stage, a chair, a pendulum, a nervous subject, and a very convincing hypnotist. Stage hypnosis is such a big draw because it has the ability to draw large crowds anywhere – whether it's in schools, bars, casinos, hotels, the sidewalk, or any other place with an audience. How and why stage hypnosis works isn't rocket science, but it mainly fashions its success from both the hypnotist and the audience.

It relies on the tremendous psychological ability of the performer, and for the part of the subject, his or her willingness to participate. As a stage hypnotist, one must be clever and keen on knowing who to select, weeding out the suspicious, the timid or shy, the neurotic, and the seemingly difficult ones.

Perhaps the most crucial part of a stage hypnotist's work is that he has to be the embodiment of confidence. Whereas the clinical hypnotist relies on his academic knowledge of the human psyche, the stage hypnotist must exhibit great showmanship, confidence, and belief. These, coupled with a "willing" subject, can all help contribute to a successful show. After all, everyone going to a stage hypnosis show is there to have a good time.

A professional hypnotist, after determining those who are willing to participate, will first gauge their level of suggestibility, that is to identify how receptive he or she will be to the suggestions laid out for them. This is a form of what we know as covert hypnosis or covert persuasion. From the use of your carefully chosen words to the pitch and tone of your voice to your body language – there are a hundred different ways to subtly give suggestions of hypnosis to a subject. These things help persuade others to follow you. In real life applications, it can be used to get someone to agree with you and do what you intended for them. Persuasiveness is the ability to make others agree with you regardless of what they believe.

Verbal techniques include knowing what you are saying. By delivering these things with sound conviction, you are convincing them that you are an expert and that you know what you are doing. This makes them abandon their fears or inhibitions. Other verbal techniques include speaking in a loud, firm voice, repeating certain actions or phrases, or making sure you get the last word when someone interrupts you.

In terms of physical techniques, you can show confidence by standing up to deliver your message, using wide hand gestures, or establishing eye contact. These things respectively represent authority, warmth and welcoming, and trust.

In a professional setting, these gestures can be effective when one is trying to make a point or to impress. It can even be made more effective when one dressed the part – looking professional and authoritative will make other people listen to you.

Going back to stage hypnosis, we must understand that being able to persuade someone can be a daunting task. Keep in mind that this someone you never know anything about, whom you've just picked out from the crowd a mere 3 minutes ago. To list down the main techniques in covert persuasion, here are a few things to keep in mind:

The main instrument for an effective covert persuasion in stage hypnosis is the use of effective language patterns and combinations of it. Practice your pre-talk, your intro, your spiel. The effectiveness of your show will depend greatly on these things.

When it comes to voter persuasion, subtlety is key. You do not let the subject become aware that he or she is being persuaded. Do not show any signs that you are targeting the subconscious. Otherwise, nothing will work. The most effective way to do this is to hide it in your conversation.

The majority of the most emotional and persuasive speeches have been made in silence, thus make sure you are both free from distraction. If one is doing this for a show or stage hypnosis, it can be a challenge, but finding ways to deviate the subject's attention away from distractions can be done easily and in so many ways. Make use of the magic words. These power words will redirect the focus to one's inner self, thereby allowing the subject to easily welcome the suggestions being presented.

Chapter 8: How to Build a Voice

Being able to build your very own, personalized hypnotic voice is an important part of making the experience with recreational hypnosis unique to both parties within that session. The hypnotic voice often becomes a part of the hypnotist's persona when they get into hypnosis. The effect that their voice has on different subjects will range from person to person, so the voice will change slightly sometimes to better fit the subject. However, the ideal hypnotic voice is one that doesn't need to be changed an incredible amount to do the job for as many hypnotic subjects as possible. That's generally the main goal for any hypnotist trying to enter the field of hypnosis and be successful—to be able to cater to as wide an audience as possible shows not only that you can be a capable hypnotist, but a flexible one as well.

Think about how your normal voice sounds to other people. Some voices have the qualities needed for ideal hypnosis already. Most voices don't—there's something dull, or obnoxious, or grating about the voice. Every single voice, however, can be influenced and improved upon to achieve the ideal result of a good hypnotic voice. The point of having a good hypnotic voice is, firstly, to be able to persuade others and to have a positive effect on those around you. Secondly, having a good hypnotic voice saves the hypnotist an enormous amount of trouble when putting a subject into trance.

As the goal of the first part of trance is finding a way for the subject to focus and relax, having a voice that is easy to listen to but not so that it takes up the entire subject's attention, is ideal. When the hypnotist has a very pleasing voice—one that's calm and softer, more droning—the subject is more easily swayed to relax and focus. However, the subject shouldn't be focusing on the hypnotist words (unless otherwise specified by that hypnotist). The wording of the hypnotist's script isn't usually very important past the initial instruction—after being told to focus, relax, close the eyes, take heavy and slow breaths, and so on, the instruction becomes repetitive and the subject often loses some of the interest in what exactly they're saying—and the sound of the hypnotist's voice alone is what carries the subject's relaxation for a lot of the remainder of the session. Additionally, the hypnotic focus of the subject usually isn't the hypnotist's voice. If it is, it often serves as a secondary focus or a tether. Often, subjects are instructed, or choose, to focus their attention on blinking, breathing, or some stationary fixture in their environment. This often serves them well; so many subjects don't rely on the words of the hypnotist too much.

However, even if you don't focus on the words of a person speaking to you, you still register their voice on some level. Although you don't pay attention to what you hear, you still hear it. When you don't pay attention to the specifics, those details quietly slip past the conscious mind and into the subconscious, where they take a much deeper hold on the subject. It's there, in the subconscious, taking deep root so that the suggestion can influence you in trance. Although that may sound scary, it's a normal part of the subconscious and it happens to us every time we hear background noise during our daily lives. Conversations we hear from others in the background of our daily activities worm their way into our subconscious mind and influence us slightly, whether we know it or not. The subconscious mind still has safeguards that prevent us from doing something ridiculous or harmful, because the conscious mind still functions most of the time, even when things slip into the backs of our heads. We're usually just pretty good at focusing and not letting ourselves be distracted by that background noise—after all, most scientists agree that if the brain paid attention to every single piece of stimulus is received, it would've long exploded by now. That noise, whatever it may be, might be something that can qualify as hypnotic-like white noise generators or looping videos of rain sounds. They're soft and droning noises with little to no variation to their sound over long periods. Therefore, much like the "proper" hypnotic voice, they're easy to focus on loosely, while being able to relax while the sound filters down to our subconscious. It's easy to listen to sounds like that since they're so droning. Because they're boring, we find ourselves relaxed by them, and often don't even realize it when we do slip away into a kind of waking trance. That kind of trance is light and very easy to break, but a deeper state of trance is achieved by the same methods. That's why usually; a hypnosis audio file will have some kind of droning noise in the background. Whether it be white noise, binaural audio, or some other kind of soft and, quite frankly, boring sound, the background music is what calms us without us even knowing it. If we only had the sound of a voice in the background, there would be something inherently unnerving about the sound, or lack thereof.

To analyze your voice is to be able to better understand the effect you can have on your subject. Most voices aren't naturally fit for the ideal hypnotist's sound, so a lot of people new to hypnosis feel discouraged by the idea of their voice not being fit for the field. While those individuals with voices naturally fit for it have a natural advantage over some of their peers, it's far from impossible to improve upon your voice to make it more suitable for your subject. While there's a certain sound to a hypnotist that automatically makes them more generally appealing to the vast majority of subjects, almost all subjects you encounter will have a slightly different idea of what a hypnotist's voice would ideally sound like. While everyone has their niches, here are a few of the more general things that many people seek out in the voice of a partner, inside of and outside of hypnosis.

Generally, subjects enjoy a lower voice, softer voice—a voice that's sultrier, even if not in a romantic sense, is any subject's perfect idea of the perfect sound. Not every subject likes a lower, deeper voice, but most people find that kind of tone alluring, if not attractive. Even in the case of a female hypnotist, most subjects enjoy a hypnotist who has a much lower vocal register. If you want to lower your voice or make it deeper to make your sound more alluring, try keeping your head lower when you speak. The main point of lowering your voice is to make you sound less anxious and more confident. Someone anxious about what they're doing raises automatic suspicion with the subject—if they don't know what they're doing and trust their skills, why should their subject? So, however, you see fit to calm yourself down and relax your body/voice, make sure that however you do it involves relaxing your body in some way. A lot of the reason we may sound anxious at times is that we tend to instinctually pitch our chins up. Notice whenever you watch a singer try to hit a note that might be too high for them, their jaw may start to drift upward. When we raise our chins higher, our vocal cords become slightly more strained and we make higher sounds. Although this works well if you're trying to achieve a higher sound, it's also not healthy for your throat, and seriously strains your vocal cords. When we lower our heads, people generally have a much lower, gruffer sound to their voice. Also, releasing all the tension from your body, especially around your chest and shoulders, will help your vocal cords to relax the following suit. With your entire body more relaxed, you find yourself less likely to raise your chin and speak anxiously. As for speaking quietly and softer, that can be more up to word choice than a physical change to your speaking. Speaking slower is generally more attractive to subjects because it makes the hypnotist seem more confident, more charismatic, and more caring. Speaking slower and softer also makes for a much more droning sound, a boring noise that's more likely to lull the subject into a trance with ease. Taking care to build the habit of speaking slowly, softly, keeping your chin lower, and making sure to keep an even tone are very small details on the surface, but they can make a massive difference in how effective your hypnotic voice is.

Some subjects like a colder voice, some like a warmer tone— this varies a significant amount from subject to subject, although many subjects you encounter will prefer a hypnotist with a very warm voice. This is an easy change to make for most, but some people have a very professional tone without intending to. If you're in a position where you want to try and change the way your voice sounds to fit the preferences of your subject, try lowering your voice when you speak to the subject. Even being quieter can make your voice sound calmer and softer if the actual words being spoken are the same. If you want a colder voice, be sure to speak a bit louder, with less of an even tone. Don't shout or speak in a way that breaks the subject's trance but adding a sharper sound to some of your words gives off a colder and more professional energy. Some subjects enjoy a hypnotist who speaks that way, as it portrays a certain level of calm confidence. However, many subjects instead prefer a softer voice as it portrays more empathy, and makes them feel more comfortable, safer.

Certain words also affect the way that we sound to different people. Everyone has different experiences that shape how they perceive different people and details, so one subject may see your voice as calm and collected, while another subject may feel threatened, in a sense, by the colder and more professional aspect of your tone. Even choosing to use different words without changing much about the way you say those words can have a massive impact on how you're perceived by your subject.

Focuses a lot more on details—using alliteration and softer adjectives allows for the subject to have a better idea of both whatever you're trying to get them to visualize, and makes that subject feel safer and much more at peace—that is if that subject takes more to a hypnotist with a softer and gentler voice. To have a more poetic take on an induction generally really helps with writing your induction which has a positive effect on your subject, more poetic writing leading to gentler and more comforting words—or colder and calmer sound, if that's what that specific subject has more of an affinity toward. Being able to use more imagery in your induction can make the difference between a satisfies subject and a subject who leaves feeling uncomfortable—that imagery is what shifts based on the knowledge that you have on your subject's preferences, to better suit them and make them feel personally much safer and more secure with you as their hypnotist. Personalizing things can mean so incredibly much to some people.

It can be hard to cater to every subject you come across, but both gaining more of an understanding of their preferences as a subject and learning to slightly change your persona with the subject you work with—as long as that shift stays within your boundaries—can help both you as a hypnotist gain experience, and help the subject feel more at peace with you as a partner. Generally speaking, the ability to be flexible and change your style for the subject you interact with is a sign that the hypnotist isn't rigid, meaning they can work with just about any different subject, really any personality type. That flexibility and ability to adapt is precisely what will put you ahead of the curve, as far as new hypnotists are concerned. The ability to grow and adapt is important in both any kind of work environment and any hobby; so whether you're looking to become a hypnotist to put bread on the table, or to simply find a space where you can have fun and enjoy yourself while meeting new people, being able to adapt to new people and a diverse range of those new people, makes moving forward in your journey a lot easier.

Chapter 9: Building the Know, Like, and Trust Factor

RAPPORT AND YOUR MINDSET ABOUT RAPPORT

Hypnotic communication and influence are all about the ability to get people to accept your suggestions and to take action on them. Before doing this, you must get them to a level where they trust you, feel safe with you, and are secure in the decisions they are making with you. The foundation is what we call the KLT factor, or the "know, like, and trust factor."

The NLP definition of rapport is getting people to feel understood by you. That is a great definition that gets straight to the point. Here's how I want you to look at this... Someone with whom you are in rapport is someone with whom you have a connection. You both can carry on a conversation for hours, and maybe it feels like you've known that person forever. Perhaps you have known them forever.

Right now, I want you to imagine somebody with whom you'd like to click naturally. Think of a person with whom you'd like to form a connection. This person can be a spouse, a family member, a love interest, or a friend. Imagine conversing with this person, and it just flows naturally. You feel like you have a deep connection with them, and you want the best for them, and they want the best for you and from you. We will call this person, Person A.

Now think of somebody who you don't click with. This person rubs you the wrong way. There's just something about them that you don't like. You feel turned off by them, and you would never listen to them or take advice from them. We will call this person, Person B.

Now imagine that you are going on vacation, and you have $5,000 in cash you need someone to look after. The banks are closed, your house is undergoing a renovation, and you need someone to look after this $5,000 in cash until you get back. Who would you trust? Who would you willingly give that to? Would you leave it with person A or person B? I bet you would rather give your money to a person you trust and feel a deep connection to.

Now, let's take it a step further. You are in the market for buying a brand-new car. Now, this is not just any car. It's your dream car. You sit down with someone, and they remind you of someone very familiar, but you're not sure who it is. You feel this deep, meaningful connection with the person, and they are genuinely passionate and interested in helping you out. However, just because you're cautious and you want to make sure you're getting the best deal, you go to a dealership down the street with the same car. The car might be a couple of hundred dollars cheaper, but this person seems like they are entirely uninterested in what you're asking for and what you want. They aren't listening to you; all they are interested in is the final sale. To take it a few steps further, they are talking trash about the dealership you were just at a couple of hours ago. They fulfill the description of a slimy used car salesperson. Who would you feel more comfortable purchasing the car from? I bet you would want to do business with the person you had that deep connection with, right?

That is what I want your mindset to be about, rapport. When we form a deep connection with somebody for whatever reason, if you wish to date them, sell them something, or become friends with them, I want you to remember this. I want you to view this transaction as two friends working together to create a common goal. And when you think of one of your close friends you click with naturally, the conversation flows you could finish each other's sentences; you would be right to assume that you have an excellent rapport with that person as they also have a great rapport with you.

Rapport is the foundation of all persuasion, influence, and connecting with people hypnotically. Once you are in rapport with the person and they are in rapport with you, you can begin influencing them and persuading them to do anything.

How to Build Rapport Quickly and Effectively

Now that you have the right mindset about rapport let's talk about how to build rapport, and also why it works so well, you will find rapport is the foundation for building a hypnotic connection with people.

The fact that makes this all come together is that people with people like themselves. Think back to that good friend you naturally click with, if they were the complete opposite of you, you probably would not click with them. But what is it that makes us feel that connection with people? It's something that we call mirror neurons. Have you ever seen someone and said to yourself, wow that person is so stylish? And then you remember that you have the same outfit you just wore the other day? Or have you ever noticed that when you're talking to a friend, you're talking at the same rate of speech, pitch, tonality, and even volume? Maybe you're both whispering, and you're close together, so you make sure you never miss a word that the other person says.

The fastest, easiest, and most efficient way to build rapport is to fire off those mirror neurons. So, how do we do that? It's quite simple. It requires that you become a little observant and flexible so you can meet people where they are. That is utilizing a technique we call matching and mirroring. Many people do this naturally, but they're not aware of it. Recognizing this and knowing when to use it can be of great value and can give you a strong persuasive advantage over others who do not know these techniques.

Matching, Mirroring, and Modeling

Some people think that matching and mirroring means copying or mimicking their target. We don't want to mimic them or copy them; we want to model them subtly. Doing this will cause those mirror neurons to fire off, and it will cause the other person to feel they connect with you because you understand them, and you are like them.

Some things we can match and mirror are postures, gestures, movements, and positioning. If you're sitting across from someone, you can sit in a similar way they are sitting. You don't have to sit exactly the way they are, but you should sit similarly. If they gesture with their right hand, you can make a similar gesture after waiting for a few beats or later in the conversation. People make a mistake by thinking they must keep up with the other person and constantly copy their gestures. Many people think that if their target moves their left hand, then they should move their left hand in the same way at the same time. However, that will get you caught, and it will turn people off instead of firing those mirror neurons.

Why Does This Work?

Words only make up 7% of our communication. That means the other 93% is all nonverbal communication. That encompasses everything from posture, to eye pattern movement, to breathing, to eye blinking, to the facial expressions we make. When we fire off those mirror neurons and model and match people, we are sending their subconscious mind signals that they can trust us, and they can be safe with us. That's why sometimes people will feel so comfortable with you they may divulge their deepest darkest secrets. Yes, with great power comes great responsibility.

The Hypnotic Handshake

Here's how a handshake can help you hypnotically connect with the person and help them feel an equal honest connection with you.

There's a lot of debate about how to shake a person's hand. I'm sure you've heard everything from shaking a person's hand with a death grip to lightly shaking a person's hand like a dead fish. In the next section, you will learn about matching, mirroring, and modeling. That's precisely what we're going to do with the handshake. When you shake someone's hand, you should match their handshake. If their handshake is firm, yours should be firm. If their grip is light, yours should also be light. That signals the subconscious mind saying, this person is like me. One other subtlety that many people miss is what you do with your facial expression when you're shaking a person's hand. Imagine you saw someone in a restaurant you have not seen in a long time, and you like this person. You would most likely be very excited to see them, and you might raise your eyebrows in surprise. Whenever your eyebrows rise, it's a signal to other people you are excited. That's how you want the person to feel whose hand you're shaking. You want to send the sign to their mind that you are excited to see them and meet them, and that you are very similar to them. However, you don't have to say that to people. They will think you are weird if you say that to them. Instead, state that in your body language by matching their handshake and raising your eyebrows as if they are a friend you haven't seen for a long time. That will send that subconscious signal that will help build rapport.

There's one more thing that I like to call the hand over hand. Some people think that when you're shaking hands with another person, that you should put your free hand over theirs. That is only socially acceptable as you are leaving the person, not when meeting or greeting the person. So, just be aware of this. Again, practice this as much as possible until it becomes natural. The idea behind this communication is that it becomes a natural thing for you to do.

FOCUSING ATTENTION ON THEM

Your ability to focus your attention on others helps you to gain a hypnotic connection. That is why it is so important to learn how to listen, ask appropriate questions, and show a sincere interest in what they do and want.

Remember, this is all about an equal and genuine connection. People don't like to hear continually, "I, I, I" or, "me, me, me." There should be a balance that shows you are interested in what they have to say, and when you show a genuine interest, they will often reciprocate and be genuinely interested in what you have to say. It can be a little difficult to develop this habit, but with practice, you'll become very aware of its power. The best way to develop this habit and technique is to become aware of how you are responding to people, and avoid saying things like, "Me too," or, "Yeah, I know," or "Good for you." Show genuine interest and ask questions that relate to what they're talking about. That will send off a connection in their mind that you genuinely care about what they're saying, you're interested in what they're saying, and it will start building that connection. Here's a sample conversation:

Them: "Hey, I just went on vacation!"

You: (Instead of saying, "Yeah, I went last week!") "Really, where did you go?"

Them: "I went to New Hampshire."

You: "Really, what did you like about New Hampshire?"

Them: "There was this store there that was cool, it was called Zeb's!"

You: "No way! Is that the store that has all of those various foods and sauces?"

Them: "Yes, and they have candy and a bunch of other fun stuff. Why, have you been?"

You: "Yes, I've been. I got a bunch of stuff there and brought it home. What did you get?"

See, in this conversation, you're putting in genuine interest, and you are relating the conversation to them in the questions you ask, but it also opens up a connection with the things in common.

Have you ever been in a conversation where you know nothing about what the other person is talking about, nor do you care? People get bored quickly if the discussion is not something, they know a lot about or are interested in. However, what gets a person to feel good and enthusiastic is when somebody listens to them about their interests. Think about this for a moment, don't you get excited when somebody talks to you about one of your interests or hobbies you have? Those are the people you want to spend more time with, right? So, what happens if someone talks about golf, and you don't like golf? Do you pretend also to be interested in the game? No! Never fake interest or pretend you have something in common. People will find out quickly that you're not genuine. Instead, just play the role of an active listener. Ask well-informed questions. People like to be the expert, so if you're asking them questions and they sit in the seat of being the expert, it will bring their energy level up, and you'll see their energy shift to being excited and enthusiastic. To shift somebody's energy, just get them talking about something that they enjoy doing.

You Have Rapport. Now What?

You have established a subconscious connection with your target. Now, this is where the real fun begins. Once you have rapport, you can start a process we call pacing and leading. Think of it as you are taking the controls now. Establishing rapport is all about meeting people on their levels of communication.

Sometimes we have to lower down to meet them where they are, and sometimes we have to rise to meet them where they are. Once those mirror neurons are fired, and we established the connection that caused the target to think, "Hey, this person is like me, and I like them because they are similar to me," we can now get them to follow us.

Once you gain rapport, they follow you. Think of it as having a conversation while running a race. You and your target both start at the same pace, and you are having a conversation while you run. Then you speed up slightly, and to keep the conversation going, the target must speed up too. Then you start slowing down, and to stay in the conversation, the target must slow down also. You are leading them to stay at your pace, but you started off running at their pace first.

When building rapport, practice it until it becomes natural and a subconscious way of communicating. You want that feeling of being in sync to be natural. To do this, you must practice with your friends, your family, strangers, and anyone and everyone you meet. However, a word of caution follows. When people feel a deep connection with you, often they will open up to you, and they will tell you things you probably don't want to or need to hear.

Once you establish rapport, you can make small adjustments to your communication styles, and the target will most likely follow you and model your communication styles. Think about ways you can use this for beneficial purposes. If you're talking to a person and they seem sad or depressed, and you want to elevate their mood, you go down to their level of communication and then work your way up to a more lighthearted way of speaking and feeling. At that point, they will follow and model your mood, your communication styles, and your positive attitude and emotions.

WHAT NOT TO DO WHEN BUILDING RAPPORT

Remember, when matching, mirroring, and modeling, we are not copying them. Some people think that they must be a carbon copy of their target. That cannot be further from the truth. For example, if you have short hair and your target has long hair and curls their hair around their index finger, don't attempt to mimic that! You'll be twirling air!

There is no need to fake interests to match theirs, and there is no need to compromise your morals, ethics, or values to try and fit in. We do not have to mesh with everyone. Never be afraid to cut off a connection or break rapport if you think there should not be a connection to be made.

Chapter 10: Using Neuro-linguistic Programming for Persuasion

When you decided to read this book on how to hypnotize someone you probably had a good reason. Perhaps you were considering being hypnotized yourself and you wanted to know more about the process. Or, maybe you have always considered a career in psychology, in particular, hypnotherapy. Then again, perhaps you read this book hoping that you could learn how to hypnotize people because you wanted to sway others to your way of thinking, to impart your will and point of view on other people. Well, with this book all things are possible.

Many people wonder if hypnosis can be used to persuade people – to win arguments, negotiate purchases, sell people things, and so on. The truth is that hypnosis truly is meant to be a therapy. That is, the field of hypnosis originated with psychologists whose goal was to help people change undesirable attitudes, fears, and behaviors. With hypnotherapy, a therapist can delve deep into a person's subconscious and reprogram how that person thinks and reacts in their waking state.

Yet there are other ways to use the subconscious.

As we discussed previously, hypnotherapy uses several different techniques. Among these are the ideas of mirroring and leading, strategies that are part of another area of psychological study called neuro-linguistic programming, or NLP, as it is commonly called. NLP is a method of changing how we communicate with others to create more favorable outcomes for yourself and those you communicate with. That is if you understand NLP you better understand how people think and behave, and you better understand how to have productive interactions with people – interactions that accomplish goals, both yours and theirs.

In this section we will talk briefly about NLP, teaching you a few concepts that you can use in your everyday life to have more beneficial interactions with other people. You can also use these tips if you go into hypnosis practice to build a better rapport with your subjects and to best help them achieve their goals.

NLP is a way of reading body language and mood and using this information to lead the other person where you want them to go. When you properly implement NLP, you can communicate better with your partner, be a better parent, work better with your colleagues, communicate more effectively with your boss, and more. When you learn NLP, you learn to know yourself better, to read what other people are thinking, and to have a direct impact on the world.

The practice of NLP has been used by psychologists and laypeople for decades. Somewhat similar to hypnosis, NLP is both an art and a science, an idea that is founded on sound observation and research, yet a skill which is developed through practice and mindfulness. Put simply, NLP is a type of subconscious programming (just like hypnosis!); it's something that we all exhibit every day. For example, if someone says something that upsets you, you may subconsciously tighten your jaw and your body muscles, staying very still as you process the information. This is a subconscious response, part of our fight or flight tendencies, which first tell your body to freeze as you access a situation.

Many therapists use NLP techniques in counseling their clients, as NLP can be a very effective way to manage phobias and anxiety. NLP counseling can also help people who have had a difficult past (perhaps with abuse or trauma) to move on and learn to manage their memories. NLP has been used by dating coaches to help instill confidence in their clients and by marketing professionals to better reach their target markets. NLP can also be used on one's self in a very simple way but with profound outcomes. Let's look at a few of the most fundamental NLP concepts, and how you can use this subconscious programming to benefit you and others in everyday life.

NLP has been used in alternative medicine to treat illnesses like Parkinson's disease. It has also been used in psychotherapy, advertisement, sales, management, coaching, teaching, team building, and public speaking. Yes, each one of these categories is a form of manipulation to some degree. You can't go to a class, the grocery store, or even a restaurant without being subject to some form of manipulation. No matter where you are you can't escape it. It's present in advertisement posters, the tactic of that business sales clerk that stops you at the mall, the product placement in the movie you're watching, and everywhere else. However, instead of being afraid of this knowledge, you can use it to your advantage and redirect that manipulation as the wielder.

But some skilled individuals can harness this power to give them an unbeatable advantage. The techniques are best used in a one-on-one or small group environment. The fewer people involved, the easier it is to read and apply NLP methods.

NLP is a complex subject and is often taught over years. That's because it takes practice to learn the range of reactions people can express. But the promise of learning people's inner secrets makes this technique especially attractive to con artists and law enforcement.

A SKILLED **NLP** USER CAN DETERMINE:

Which side of the brain their subject uses

People fall along a spectrum between creative and analytical. New science shows that brain function is distributed across the brain. But it is still helpful to think of people through this lens. Word choice, sentence structure, and associations all reveal details about the person that uses them. Left-brained people often use words that elicit emotions or experiences. Right-brained people like to include things outside their experience or expertise.

Which sense is most important to them

We have more than the five senses (sight, sound, taste, touch, and smell) most people know about. We also have a sense of order, balance, morality, and a host of others, and each of us has one or two that are more important than the rest.

How their brain stores information.

Our brains are the most complex computers we have ever come across. They store and process billions of bits of information a second. Each one functions a little differently. One of the biggest areas of divergence is in how people store information.

Some individuals have a memory like a sponge, soaking up everything near them. Others are more like a strainer that catches big chunks and allows everything to pass through. NLP techniques help people discern the difference and to what degree.

Over time, NLP users get better at keeping track of information. With enough time, users can improve their information tracking abilities to near-genius levels. This gives us an advantage over anyone who isn't as experienced or naturally gifted.

When they are lying or making things up.

People perform specific behaviors when they make things up called "tells." NLP users like me can pick up on these tells and be able to call out the liar as they lie. Some people are better than others at lying but everyone has at least one tell.

Skilled liars understand that for someone else to believe their lie, so must they. So they convince themselves of it first. They often don't display all the signs of dishonesty because they truly believe the lie as they tell it.

Practice can help people fall for their lie but the process demands a selective memory. This feature is more reliably detected than the oft-cited slight downward glance. It also proves to be a more consistent indicator of ingrained deception than awkward looks. Power imbalances also make a refusal to make eye contact less reliable as well.

How to make someone drop their guard.

When someone likes you, they want to include you in their lives. Listening to what they say often provides deep insight into what controls their lives. People offer up their darkest secrets willingly, believing that I truly understand them.

How you can condition people without their consent/knowledge.

Let's face it, people don't like finding out someone was manipulating them. It violates the idea that we are in control of our lives. But sometimes the truth is hard to take, and we need someone to help us see the way without calling us out on it.

We all manipulate those around us to one degree or another. This can be as simple as breaking a bad habit or establishing new relationship rules with a toxic family member. By steering them in the right direction, we can help them respond to how we prefer.

NLP doesn't brainwash someone (that's covered elsewhere) or cause them to do something out of character. But it does reveal the strings that control each of us. What you do with those strings once you have them is up to you.

LISTEN AND WATCH

This is the most time-consuming step, as it is the basis of building the structure for the more intimate relationship you'll build later. Body language is essential to NLP practices. Not only is it vital to the beginning, but, knowing how to read body language comes into play throughout the NLP process and any other psychological process. Luckily, the longer you build a relationship with someone, the easier it will be to know their tells, as they are developed from habit. Some people may be guarded around you, which will appear as tense or straight shoulders and back, not holding your gaze, or even fidgeting.

This is a sign you aren't building a vital rapport. Before moving any further, this person needs to feel relaxed and warm around you. Watch for an open face, a relaxed smile, and some easy-going interaction such as light laughter. Stay away from heavy topics until this person is comfortable with you.

BUILDING RAPPORT WITH OTHERS

Every day we use our communications to try and influence others. Unfortunately, most of us are rarely successful because we don't know what we are doing – we don't understand the psychology of other people and we don't know how to get into another person's subconscious mind. But by reading this book you are taking significant steps towards developing that understanding.

One important aspect of getting on well with others is the building of rapport. First, let's consider what rapport is. Rapport is simple, it is the magic that happens when two people are getting along really well and communicating on the same level. When you have a rapport with another person you are each understanding the other, you are listening better, and you are accomplishing something.

You do not have to think the same way as another person or agree with everything they say to have rapport. You simply have to be communicating similarly. One way that people show rapport is when they mirror each other, that is to say, they have similar body language. People who have a good rapport use a similar body language including posture and eye contact. Imagine in your head that you are talking and laughing with a friend. Likely, you are both standing with your feet a comfortable width apart, your arms moving animatedly as you speak, you are both smiling, and your eyes make frequent contact. You have a good rapport. But what if the other person suddenly stops smiling, crosses their arms over their chest, and starts to avoid your eyes? Immediately you should know that something is wrong, that something has changed, and that this person no longer feels connected to you – you are no longer in rapport.

Practicing effective NLP means being aware of these types of changes in the other person and knowing how to respond to them positively.

Mirroring body language is not only a way to show that we are naturally in rapport with another person – it is a way to build rapport as well. When you are talking to a person whom you feel uncomfortable with, or whose discomfort you sense, you need to work on your rapport. You can do this through mirroring and then leading.

MIRRORING

Mirroring, as we noted briefly above, is the practice of having a similar body language. Mirroring is not about mimicking or copying negatively, it is about showing that you are "on the same page", as they say, as the other person, that you are in sync.

When you mirror someone you match their body language, stance, eye contact, vocal tone, and so forth. Let's consider one way that we do this all of the time: say that you are a trainer, it is your job to go into a business after a salesperson has made the sale and to train the staff on the new equipment that their company just purchased. If you want to build a good rapport with those you are training the first thing you should do is find out how they dress and mirror them. You would not want to go into a fancy bank, where everyone is wearing business suits, dressed in jeans and a t-shirt. However, you also should not go into an auto service station, where everyone is wearing jeans and dirty t-shirts, in a business suit. When your clothes are this mismatched to those you are communicating with you are not in sync and it makes it more challenging to build rapport. Thus, you should dress appropriately to where you are going.

This same type of synching goes for other things:

If you walk into a meeting and everyone is sitting down, you will build the best rapport if you, too, sit down.

If you are talking with a group of people who are laughing and gesturing, you should match this body language if you want to fit in.

We mirror people every day... We do this when we hear someone's sad news and automatically lower our tone and volume in response. We do this when someone tells us good news and we cheer or our voice becomes higher in pitch. But for mirroring to be truly effective you cannot rely solely on your subconscious – you must use your conscious mind to recognize how you want to interact with another person and alter your body language as necessary.

Rapport is not about an agreement in content, it is about an agreement in body language. It is also about respecting that others have a right to their opinion and thus choosing your words carefully. If you tell a person, "Yes, I hear what you are saying, and I think this…" you are building great rapport. Yet, if you change just one word you can break that rapport, for example, "But, you don't understand…" – that but changes everything. You have just broken your rapport; use the word and instead. When you mirror the behavior of others and choose your words positively you build a bridge that helps you to communicate more effectively.

LEADING OTHERS WHERE YOU WANT THEM TO GO

After you have built a rapport with a person you can use another concept, called leading, to take them mentally down a path where you wish to go. This is where NLP starts to show you how to influence others. Leading is about both what you say and how you say it. When you lead, you alter your behavior in a way that encourages the other person to follow you; as they follow your behavior, so they follow your ideas.

The best way to illustrate the power of leading is to think of an argument.

Imagine that you are fighting with your partner or a friend. The conversation started pleasantly, but somehow it changed and slowly you have seen your partner become more and more upset. Now, your partner is speaking in a loud, angry voice. Their arms are crossed tightly over their chest, their jaw and shoulders are tense. You want to diffuse this argument and bring it back to a productive conversation.

Most of us know that telling a person to calm down usually upsets them more than it calms them. So, let's try something else. First, you match your partner's stance. You cross your arms, tighten your jaw and shoulders, and raise the tone and volume of your voice. You do this for a moment, but then you bring your voice down in volume, and you ease out the tone. Still keeping your arms crossed, mirroring your partner, you bring your voice to a normal, conversational level and tone. Then, slowly, you loosen your shoulder and jaw muscles, and finally, you uncross your arms slowly and take on a more casual, open stance. Most likely you will see your partner do the same thing. Unconsciously they will follow your lead, lowering their voice, unfolding their arms and calming down. Few reasonable people can continue to yell and be angry in the face of calm; this is a tactic that most often works.

You can use leading like this in many settings. You can lead a sad person to be a bit happier if you match their sadness, but then slowly come around to a sunnier disposition (of course, this won't work with anyone who is clinically depressed). You can lead an overly excited person to calm down by matching their excitement and then leading them into calm. The list goes on and on.

You can even lead a person to your point of view by repeating their words and then leading them to your ideas. For example, you might say, "So, you are saying that your company is doing well with your current software, yet you feel that new software might up sales even further. It sounds like it would be worth your while to hear a bit about my company's software package." The point is that when you understand people when you build a rapport with them, and when you know how to reach the subconscious, you can make a difference in how people think and behave.

USING NLP ON YOURSELF

As we have only hinted at, NLP is a very powerful subconscious tool that can help you communicate better with others. However, NLP can also help you to help yourself in some very tangible ways.

Let's begin our conversation about how you can change your attitudes and actions by considering the power of belief. If you have studied or observed the human condition at any length you know that what a person believes is one of the most powerful influences on their outcomes. This is why a person must be open to hypnotism to be hypnotized – if they do not believe that hypnosis can help them than likely it cannot; if you want to know how to hypnotize someone, you have to understand this. People who expect to be successful are more successful. People who believe that they can achieve. People who feel that they have bad luck, or are destined to fail, will fail. The power of belief is almost absolute.

One example of the power of belief comes from a groundbreaking study in education:

We use this power of affirmative belief every day. You use it when you tell your children that you know they can read that next word or figure out that math problem, you do it when you encourage your coworker to lead a team, telling them, "You can do it." We even use it when we cheer and rally for our favorite sports teams. Every day we use affirmative positive thinking to influence outcomes.

The great news is that you can use this power of belief to influence your subconscious as well.

That means that you can program yourself to be successful. You may have heard of this as it has been all over popular media in recent years in a book called The Secret. But the truth is that there is no secret, there is just the power of the mind.

What The Secret talks about is the Law of Attraction, the idea that we attract that which we expect and talk or think about. If you think about being wealthy, you attract wealth. However, if you think about how poor you are all of the time then you simply attract poverty. Does this mean that magic happens, that if you think about money then the money fairy stuffs dollar bills under your pillow? No. While the book The Secret may make it sound mystical, the truth is that the Law of Attraction is about subconscious programming.

When you think about something all of the time you become obsessed with it, that is the idea becomes deeply embedded. When you become obsessed with something it works its way into your deepest subconscious and your brain will start to act in a way that brings it into the conscious mind by making it happen. We think of obsession as a bad thing, but if you are obsessed with something good there is nothing wrong with it at all.

Let's look at the issue of being overweight. If you constantly think about how fat you are, that you feel unhealthy, that you look terrible, your brain starts to internalize this. Your subconscious mind will grow to think of itself as fat and it will keep you fat by making poor food choices.

However, if you reprogram your mind and you start to think about how great you feel, how all those vegetables you eat are giving you energy, how you feel fit and thin, your subconscious will start to work towards that. This is how hypnosis works! You know this because you know how to hypnotize someone now.

In hypnosis for weight loss, the hypnotist plants these same thoughts directly into the subconscious, telling the subconscious to think like a thin person, to be thin, to do. With NLP you simply take a different route, implanting these ideas into your subconscious by thinking about them consciously, over and over. Many people do this by creating a vision board, that is a poster where they put pictures of what they wish to accomplish; then they look at those pictures many times, day after day, implanting those goals into their subconscious.

Another NLP concept that is also used in hypnotherapy is the idea of the anchor. An anchor starts with the mental preparation that we just described and goes a bit further. In short, and the anchor is some action, word, or item that reminds you of something else.

From building rapport with others to reprogramming yourself, NLP is a powerful tool that you can use in daily, waking life. While the focus of this book is on hypnosis, we needed to present some of these ideas to give you a more well-rounded view of the abilities of the subconscious mind. You may wish to do more research on the topic if you would like to learn more about how you can use NLP to influence and better interact with people daily in the waking world.

Chapter 11: Persuasive Hypnotic Language

Now we get to the part that people often associate with forming hypnotic connections with hypnotic language. As I said previously, the words we use only compose 7% of the way we communicate. So, let's make those words as powerful and impactful as possible. You'll also learn that it's not just what you say, but how you say it.

Hypnotic persuasive language bypasses the critical and analytical part of the mind so what you say is not analyzed.

Let's look at some words and phrases that can have a dramatic impact on your target's ability to trust you, believe you, and accept what you say is accurate. The hypnotic words I will teach you are called truisms. Some words have social and emotional proof to them, so they become challenging for people to deny. When you use these words in sentences and your communication with people, often, what you say after these words, the target must accept as truth. You can use these words in sales, with a spouse or partner, and even with strangers to allow you to cut in front of them in a long line.

Most people: This hypnotic phrase "most people" is a powerful one. Whatever comes after the phrase, "most people" is not analyzed by the conscious mind, and it goes right into the subconscious mind. This phrase works because it plays on our psychological needs and insecurities. If we disagreed with "most people," then it plays on our insecurities of being left out. As humans, we don't like to be left out, but if we are left out of what most people do, say or think, then we can have feelings of isolation and loneliness. Therefore, it is easier to agree to what follows this statement. Let's look at some examples of how this technique can be used.

"Most people who tell me what you just told me will choose this option here."

"Most people in your situation would use this."

"Most people who know what you know will make a decision now."

This technique is used best when you want to get people to decide on something or make a specific choice. You can help them narrow down their selection and then lead them to choose the best option for them. Using this strategy will get them to think they made that choice all on their own, and that option they picked is the best one.

A variation of most people is to say something like, "If you are like me, and like most people, then…"

Everyone knows/everyone says: This one works based on the same concept as most people. The psychological thought process here is "if everyone knows this, then I must know this too because I am a part of everyone!" This technique works well with commonly known phrases and truisms (see below) that are difficult to deny.

"Everyone knows the early bird catches the worm…"

THE THREE POWERFUL WORDS THAT BUILD A DEEP CONNECTION

Just as building rapport through matching, mirroring, and modeling is important; using these three magic words is also amazingly effective.

Feel, Felt, found: That gets your target into a more agreeable state and makes them feel understood by you. Here is another example. "I know how you feel, that it seems too expensive; many people I have worked with have felt the same way when they first hear the fee, but then when they experienced results right away, they found that they were happy that they made a decision right away and that it was very inexpensive for what they were getting."

"That's funny! I know how you feel, I have a friend who is just like this girl that you're talking about, and when she kept acting like a 'mean girl,' some of her good friends wouldn't talk to her anymore. Is that what happened to your friend?" Notice how we didn't have to use the three words exactly, (feel, felt, found), but it has the same effect.

Using this technique can help you relate to people on a deeper level and help them feel like you understand them. Once you have this connection, you can recommend solutions, and they will be more open to listening to you.

EMBEDDED HYPNOTIC COMMANDS

Embedded hypnotic commands are hidden commanding phrases that prompt your target to take action without having the target realizing you are telling them to do something. An example can be something like this "As you're sitting here, and we are having this conversation about wanting to go into hypnosis now... you may find that the things I say are very easy to achieve." The embedded command is "go into hypnosis now." This command is not analyzed by the conscious mind because it's hidden amongst other words.

These embedded commands don't just have to be in the spoken language; they can be in text format, as well. People often ask if it's possible to be hypnotized by reading something. Yes, you can. It happens all the time. We often "trance out" when reading, and we put ourselves in the world that the author is trying to convey to us.

Example: "A few weeks ago, I texted my friend and wanted her to call me" The text read "You can call me if you want to hear what happened." There are two embedded commands here. One is, "you can call me" and the other is, "you want to hear what happened."

Here are some other examples of really crafty embedded suggestions. Again, please remember that these may seem obvious, but I promise you, they sound so natural when you use them, that they are not heard by the conscious mind. They are heard and given meaning by the subconscious mind.

What if you could get people to feel they like you from the very beginning? Here is a way to do this using embedded hypnotic commands.

"You, like me, _____."

We are telling the target they like us without telling them they like us. It sounds like this, "You (pause), like me (pause), understand the true value of these techniques." Again, the subconscious applies one meaning to what you are saying while the conscious mind hears something that has a different meaning. However, the subconscious meaning will always win over. Remember, the subconscious is the automatic and natural part of the mind; and what gets in there sticks.

Here are two great ways to make this technique even more powerful. As you are saying, "You, like me..." gesture in towards yourself, bringing the attention towards you, and at the same time, slightly nod your head yes. That will send even more subtle nonverbal cues to the subconscious mind. Powerful? You bet!

By now (buy now)

The same principles are applied where the conscious mind hears one thing, but the subconscious mind hears another and applies that information to your automatic responses. That is great to use when selling something and you want to condition them to be ready to buy. When you say something like, "By now, we have reviewed all of the options, and you must be ready to make a decision." Or something like, "Now you know all of the features, so by now, I'm sure you must be ready to make a decision." What we mean by saying these statements is a time reference "by now." However, what the subconscious mind hears is "BUY now!" Interesting, isn't it?

RECOGNIZING THESE TECHNIQUES

Many people do not realize how much and how often they are being persuaded to act, behave, or react in a certain way. Advertisers, marketers, politicians, and even religious figures and institutions are continually using powers of persuasion to try and get us to act in a certain way or even believe what they want us to believe. To become aware of these techniques, watch commercials, and look at advertisements and look for embedded commands and hypnotic language such as the words we were going over previously. By doing this, you can easily become aware of how you may be persuaded without even realizing it. Once you recognize these techniques and how they are used, you can resist against them, or at least be more aware if you are acting on your own free will, or if your decisions, beliefs, and behaviors are being influenced.

"You could either _____, or _____?"

"Would you rather _____, or _____?"

These are great leading phrases when presenting options or choices. It's what we call an assumptive question. That assumes that they will choose one of the two options you are offering. That works well when setting appointments with people "you could either come in on Tuesday at 9:00 am or Thursday at 2:00 pm." It also works great when choosing between two price points. "You could either choose the $3,700 program or the $5,300 program." Again, you are assuming that they are choosing one of the two.

You can use this one for a spouse as well. "Honey, would you rather have Italian or Chinese food tonight?" Just be careful, when your spouse catches on, they may say, "Neither, I want Mexican!"

That is also an effective technique to use on your children when you want them to go to bed. "Jake, do you want to go to bed now, or in ten minutes?" You are making them think they have the freedom of choice. Little do they know, it's all in your hands.

"I wonder..."

You may notice that some of the language we have been using is vague and some are open-ended. A lot of hypnotic communication is letting people come to their conclusions. Even though you are leading them, they will still think that their thoughts, ideas, and "choices" are free will. Little do they know; you are leading them exactly where you want them to go. The words "I wonder" will cause your target to think about what you are saying and see your side of things.

"I wonder if you'll see my point of view."

"I wonder what if you'll be able to see the bright side of this."

"I wonder if you'll end up dumping your boyfriend and go out with me instead." (I had to sneak that one in there.)

Chapter 12: Direct Suggestion Hypnosis

This method can be used successfully as long as its use is in accordance with the issues the client is dealing with. For a direct suggestion to work, it must be used to touch on the subject's core belief system. Every suggestion must be specific to the subject. This will make him a lot more responsive and accepting.

It is also important for direct suggestions to be delivered authoritatively. However, the suggestions may also be delivered gently like in a casual conversation. Still, direct suggestions may be inserted in a story or metaphors. No matter how the suggestions are delivered, they should follow the most important rule. That is the suggestions must be completely relevant to the subject, targeting his core belief system directly. Direct suggestion hypnosis technique works by planting concepts directly into the person's mind. The world is represented in a human being's mind by images. This is why whenever he hears a word, he must first access memories related to that word before he can understand that word. The effectiveness of direct suggestion lies in the fact that it may be used to target a person's specific issues. This means that for it to be effective, the hypnotist must first know some facts about the subject. When the hypnotist can hit the correct spot, it increases the chance that the suggestion will be accepted by the individual.

The mind works in such a way that what the person visualizes, he obtains. The suggestions provided in hypnosis create powerful images for the individual. When health or anything positive is suggested during hypnosis the subconscious works to turn it into reality.

USING DIRECT SUGGESTIONS
Repetition

The more a direct suggestion is repeated to the person, the more effective it becomes. However, be careful about repeating the same words. The key is in finding many different ways on how to present the same idea. It may be repeated in various parts of the session.

Correct: "You like your job. Your job provides you with a sense of satisfaction. Your work brings out the best in you. Your occupation provides you with a sense of purpose. You enjoy learning new things while you work. Your job enables you to grow as a person."

Wrong: "From now on, you will love your job."

Notice that in the sample script, the same thought converses in different ways. It also provides reasons for loving a job. It targets specific core beliefs like the need for personal growth, satisfaction, sense of purpose and direction, etc.

Positive Wording

An important thing to remember when using direct suggestion is that your words must conjure images of things that the subject wants. If you're not careful with your words, you might end up invoking the opposite.

Correct: "You enjoy being with people and talking with them. You are confident whenever you are in a crowd."

Wrong: "You are no longer afraid of people. You no longer feel nervous when you are speaking in front of a huge crowd. You no longer worry that they will judge you. You're no longer afraid that they will see through you and think you are a fraud."

Psychiatrists use positive phrasing for a reason. Negative words paint a negative picture. For instance, if you tell someone that he should not be afraid of people, the mere mention of fear makes that person nervous. You can tell the person to not think about being judged, but he will only feel overwhelmed with images of people judging him. In other words, you (although unintentionally) help enforce the same things that you want that person to forget about by using negative wording. This is why it is important to create positive imagery using positive statements like the first example does.

Take it to the Present

When using direct suggestions, be sure to deliver the idea in the present tense. Suggest to the subconscious that it is now part of the person's present life and not something that is in the distant future. When you suggest in the future tense, you're risking the chance that it may never occur.

Correct: "You can sleep well at night."

Wrong: "You will be able to sleep well soon."

This is another important thing. The suggestion can become more real to the person if you make him feel like it is happening now. You eliminate a chance of it not coming true because it is already happening as you speak.

Reflection

The direct suggestion should be able to reflect the subject's experience.

Correct: "You exhibit confidence in everything that you do, from greeting a stranger to parking your car."

Wrong: "You exhibit confidence as you perform in front of everyone. (This is not relevant unless the person plays an instrument, or acts, or sings, etc. in public)

When using the direct suggestion method, it is important to know something about the person. You can craft direct suggestions according to his personal experiences. Although the second example is phrased beautifully, it is not relevant to everyone and it may not be to your subject. You have to be specific to the subject's experiences so it will help to get to know them first.

Do you ever wonder why it's much easier to convince a friend rather than a stranger? It's because you know your friend. You know how to get through to them because you are familiar with their experiences. You can make effective suggestions by being familiar with the subject's life.

The Subject's Beliefs

To increase its effectiveness, it is necessary to base the suggestion on the person's beliefs. For instance, if the subject believes in karma, then tell him that success in life is their positive karma. Use metaphors so that the person will be able to relate to what you are suggesting.

Correct: "The universe's reward for you is success. You are on your way there. As of this moment, confidence is building within you. You are ready to change. You are willing to change. You are ready to take what is yours."

Wrong: "There is no such thing as karma. You achieve success when you go after it and grab it."

Beliefs are important to everyone. Getting to know your subject's core belief system is not only important in crafting effective direct suggestions. It is also essential in avoiding direct suggestions that may contradict his belief system. The moment you deliver a suggestion that goes against his core beliefs, you run the risk of losing his responsiveness to your words.

Focus

Effective direct suggestion requires dealing with one issue at a time. For example, a person is suffering from both gambling addiction and insomnia. It is best to address these problems in two separate sessions because each suggestion in each session must be meant to support each other.

Correct: "You can sleep well at night. While sleeping, your body can recharge itself so that when you wake up in the morning, you feel happy and energized."

Wrong: "You can sleep well at night and you can resist gambling. You no longer feel the urge to smoke."

The fact is it is quite impossible to address all issues at once. Do not rush the process. If you want to be as effective as possible, you have to focus on one specific issue at a time.

Be Thorough

As much as possible, it is necessary to address every possible aspect of the issue. Instead of suggesting a complete solution, there should be a series of suggestions that support each other and eventually leads towards a solution.

Correct: "You speak with confidence. Your voice is steady and firm. You look at people directly in the eyes when you talk to them. You can communicate your feelings. You walk with confidence. You are aware that each stride has a purpose. With the confident way in which you move, you are showing the world that you are a worthwhile person." Wrong: "You are always confident when you're around people."

Remember to cover all your bases. Do not leave any stone unturned. Ask yourself what issues this person is facing. What kind of situations had he been through concerning each issue? Make sure you include them in your suggestions. In other words, you must go through each issue thoroughly.

The Subject's Experience

Use the person's experiences so that he will be able to relate more with the suggestion. For example, if he mentioned that he had won an amateur poetry contest, then take advantage of that information in delivering your suggestion.

Correct: "You can feel the confidence building inside you. It's that very same feeling that you have felt when you won that poetry competition. That time when you were able to show everyone how well you write and how skilled you are in communicating your feelings…"

Wrong: "You must have achieved something in the past that you are proud of. Gain confidence from that moment."

Use the subject's experiences, both negative and positive, to reinforce the suggestions. Help your subject celebrate his successes. It is a huge confidence booster that contributes to motivation so he can achieve what he wants to whether it is losing weight, overcoming social phobia, or quitting smoking.

Emphasizing the Subject's Assets

Often, individuals are unaware of what they have. They tend to overlook and belittle their resources. Use the person's background to identify possible areas of strength. For example, the subject has revealed to you a particular job crisis that he had to solve by himself. By mentioning this, you can remind him of his capabilities.

Correct: "Remember that time when you had that incident at work. You were able to deal with the problem singlehandedly. This shows that you can think straight and to prioritize during crises."

Wrong: "Try searching for any resources from within you. Perhaps you know of a personal strength..."

Be Realistic

Any suggestions made must be achievable by the individual. They must be positive, and they must stretch the person's possibilities but they must also be realistic and in line with a person's capability. Remember that the subject may be able to reject a suggestion if he wishes to and any suggestion that seems unattainable will automatically be rejected by his subconscious.

Correct: "You respect your body. You can control what you eat. You can prepare healthy, well-balanced meals and enjoy eating them in moderation. You are on your way towards experiencing its gradual positive effects on your body."

Wrong: "You will lose weight this week. You will start looking attractive and everyone will begin to notice you and your transformation."

Avoid Suggestions Set up for Failure

Some hypnotists make the mistake of being careless with their words. Avoid using absolutes like "never", "always", and "all the time". Otherwise, your suggestion is meant to fail from the very beginning. Be sure to match the suggestion according to each individual's lifestyle and capability.

Correct: "You can find time in dedicating yourself towards your goal. You can use the tiny spurts of energy in between chores to work on your goal."

Wrong: "You will work on your goal every day. You will dedicate all of your time towards achieving your goal." (A busy person's subconscious is likely to automatically reject this suggestion.)

Engage the Senses

Keep in mind that each individual can experience the world in his unique way. To form a big impact, you must be sure to engage all of the person's senses during hypnosis. For instance, limiting yourself to visual metaphors is unlikely to work on a subject that is unable to visualize very well.

Correct: "Imagine yourself in that party. You see the people looking at you. They notice your confidence. They see your smile and they smile back. You hear them greeting you. You hear the soft music playing in the background and you know that you're going to have a good time."

Focus on the Subject's Behavior

You should always bear in mind that the suggestions are meant only to influence the individual's behavior. Making suggestions that involve the behavior of other people is misleading and is likely to result in disappointment.

Correct: "Every day, you do something to prove to your children that you deserve their respect. You earn their respect by providing for them. You communicate openly with your children. You show them that they have your support."

Wrong: "Your children have accepted you for what you are. They love you and they respect you."

Use Strong Emotions

Suggestions work better when the behaviors are related to powerful emotions.

Correct: "When you open your eyes, with each second, your concentration increases. Your mind grows more focused. Your vision is sharp. Your body feels alive. Something is stirring from within you. It's a feeling of anticipation for the new day. The new 'you' is ready to face the new day."

Wrong: "When you wake up, you will feel recharged."

Support Suggestion with Logic

Subjects can receive suggestions better if they are supported by reason. However, keep in mind that the mind under hypnosis does not have the ability for full critical thinking so what's needed here is implied hypnotic logic.

Correct: "You have spent enough time observing other people's lives. Now it's time to work on yours. And when you think of all the successes of those other people that you know, think of how you deserve the same thing. And think of how you can achieve that success when you stop drinking. You can stop drinking today."

Wrong: "You can stop drinking today."

Simplicity is the Key

Speaking to the mind in its subconscious state is like talking to the mind of a child. Make sure that you choose words that are simple, short, and direct and those that create the most impact. If you use long and complex sentences, your words are likely to be ignored.

Correct: "You want to be happy. You want to make your family happy. You want to save money. You are ready to let go of your gambling habits."

Wrong: "Habitual gambling can cause serious detrimental effects on an individual's personal and social life. You will see a marked increase in your finances and an improvement in your social relationships if you decide to abstain from gambling."

Chapter 13: Advanced Hypnosis

You have hopefully gotten a host of ideas on how to do direct hypnosis, from induction to suggestion. Now, we will take you into some advanced techniques that you can bring into your toolbox to help people create the changes that you want them to create. In this section, we will talk about conversational hypnosis and indirect suggestion, pattern interrupts, Cold-Warm-Hot Reading, parts therapy, and more. If you do not know what some of these things are, you will by the end of this chapter, and you will have some immediate strategies to get results with them.

Each of these powerful tools will reveal to you the depth that hypnosis can be used in every aspect of your life. Whether you are looking to do it in a therapeutic sense, or looking to persuade, influence, or control someone in the outside world. These fun and amazing techniques are simple and yet very powerful.

INDIRECT SUGGESTION AND CONVERSATIONAL HYPNOSIS

An indirect suggestion was started and mastered by Milton Erickson, who became world-renowned for his ability to help clients with seemingly innocuous conversations. What indirect suggestion is exactly what its name suggests, a process of weaving suggestions without a person aware that you are making a suggestion. Entire books have been written to the process, but we will focus on some of the amazing language tools you can use to immediately embed a suggestion to people. Using indirect suggestions can be incredibly powerful and the levels that you can take it too when you know what you are doing can be amazing. There are stories of Milton Erickson sitting at tables with friends and talking to them and they'd find themselves handing him salt, or pepper, or a drink without ever being asked, and only realizing that he was playing with their mind, embedding commands into his language to get them to take those actions. Now, I can't show you that level of Jedi Wisdom, but we learn instant hacks into people's minds.

The first and most obvious is the word, "Because." This secret has not been a secret for a long time and yet most people still do not know the power of the word because probably because few people spend time studying how to use their language powerfully. Anyways, this has been statistically proven to be a powerful tool to get people to take action. In an experiment made famous by Robert Cialdini in his amazing and revelatory book Influence some several decades ago, a group of psychologists working in a school shut down one of the copier machines so that a line would start.

The next powerful statements are If/Then statements or equivalency statements as they are called. If you are reading this book, then you are getting an education in hypnosis, persuasion, and the dark secrets of psychology. If/then allows you to equivocate anything and as we talked about with the power of correlation and causation, the brain is always looking for these types of things. So, because of that, oftentimes these types of statements are just accepted.

Now, one of the most powerful political tools used by our current president is one powerful statement, "Many people say…" This is a plea to social pressure. It is a powerful way of giving creed to your opinion and strengthening the way people think about what you are telling them. It makes it acceptable. Many people say that when they believe that a lot of people hold an opinion, it gives the opinion more credibility. There are other ways of phrasing it as well. "I read a study somewhere," "I heard once," "The news was saying," and so on and so on… Each of these holds the unique power and attribute to give people a chance to appreciate what you are saying without having to judge you as the source.

Finally, an important and lawyerly process is the use of presuppositions. Imagine a prosecutor comes up to the defendant to question them and asks them, "Did you beat your wife that day?" If the defendant says, "No," they have opened the door for the prosecutor to lean in on accusations that he did beat his wife. Presuppositions are statements that presuppose the action ahead of time within the question. You would be amazed at how well these work. "Whenever you buy the car, you're going to need x," says to the person that they will buy the car. This might feel like some sort of cheap ploy, but in truth, these small weaved together suggestions, really do build a canvas in the minds of people that they can fully appreciate and take action because of.

PATTERN INTERRUPTS

Imagine that you are sitting in a room with a friend and you are having a conversation with a friend when suddenly you get thirsty, so you get up, walk into the kitchen, and get a drink. Suddenly when you get back to the couch, your brain is blank on what you were talking about. You have no idea what you were saying and what others were saying. What happened? Your memory is not bad that is not the problem. What happened is that your brain can only process so much information, so when it processes that information, such as the conversation, but suddenly gets met with a different stimulus, like a change of room, suddenly the information of the conversation is pushed from the mind. That's what a pattern interrupt is.

Whenever something interrupts or undermines our expectations, it causes the pattern we were expecting to be interrupted and creates a state of confusion. In this section, I will show you exactly what you need to do to use pattern interrupts for your benefit, whether it is for yourself or to use on someone else.

The Pattern Interrupt, when mastered and understood, gives you everything that you need to allow you to break through people's resistances. It gives you the ability to stop your negative thought patterns in their place. The best thing is that it works regardless of the resistance that people will throw up, as it is meant to confuse, and tear down those barriers of resistance.

I am guessing that you have probably had moments in your life as if everyone has when your brain drifted off into some negative territory and affected the rest of your day. It happens to all of us occasionally. Life has its ways of bringing negative emotions to the front of our minds. Sometimes it is part of the programming we developed throughout our lives. Sometimes it has to do with the fact that we have a bad way of looking at things and processing things in our lives. Other times, it is simply because we have been left to the mental prowess that we have at any moment. It is so easy for emotions to take us over and to control our lives. Whether it is anger or sadness, misery, or rage, negative emotions have their way of taking us over and controlling us. However, our emotions do not need to be like that. They do not need to rule us, they do not need to dominate us, and they do not need to control us. No. When you understand how to break these patterns of thinking and alter your thinking, you can take greater control of your life... and better yet, you can help others get out of their negative path as well.

You will be amazed at how powerful pattern interrupts can be when you fully learn them. You will discover how you can alter others and yourself.

The testament to the power of Pattern Interrupts lies in their ability and their versatility. Their ability to so easily be used across the board: from psychology and hypnotherapy to interrogation and sales, pattern interrupts can be utilized to get results faster than anything else does. And the best thing is that there are not a series of steps or anything like that when it comes to mastering pattern interrupts, there are just a few solid principles that you need to understand, and then you will be good to go. The greatest advertisers, marketers, salespeople, and therapists know how to use pattern interrupts to get the best results possible, and they do, often, and consistently.

So, what are the principles of making pattern interrupts work? All pattern interrupts occur from a deviation from other's expectations. What does that mean? If someone sticks there to hand out at you, how many times do you reach out to shake it? Do you even think about shaking their hand, or do you just understand the expectation that when someone offers their hand, you are to reach out and shake it as part of the process? There was a hypnotist and mentalist, who wanted to show the power of pattern, interrupts, so he walked up to a counter at the DMV where a woman was sitting waiting to take his information. When it came to his phone number, he did not give the number in the same 3-3-4 structure that we usually give out our phone number. Instead, he broke it up into 2-1-3-2-1-1-1 at the end, then, when he finished, he announced, "I'm thirsty, could you get me a water from the staff fridge?" and without thinking she got up and started doing it. Now, why did this happen? When her brain had to process something outside of her expectations, it overloaded the conscious mind, the gatekeeper that we talked about with hypnosis 101. With the gatekeeper overwhelmed, her unconscious mind was left unguarded, and with that, a basic suggestion made its way into her mind.

When the brain is met with something that confuses it or overwhelms it, the brain begins the process of shutting down to process things. The brain is constantly trying to process everything that it encounters, but your consciousness is only able to process so much before it needs to take a break. To process everything, your whole brain needs to become more efficient, to become more efficient, it needs to create shortcuts that the brain can use to make everything easier and simpler.

All of this is to say that when you can subvert the natural expectations that someone has, you can easily begin to interrupt their current emotional states, and their current way of thinking, giving you the exact opportunity needed to go about and take control of the conversation. Think about it, people expect that when they say to a salesperson that they are just looking around, that that will end the interaction with the salesperson. I would bet some of you have become so used to saying that to salespeople, that when they approach you, even when you are looking for something, you still say no. That is why the best salespeople in the world are those who can respond to objection and know how to approach a person with offers that do not at first appear like offers. Though, this subverting of expectations is so powerful that it is used during interrogations. Radical fighters in Iraq when apprehended oftentimes expected to be tortured. They were indoctrinated to believe that capture meant torture. So, when an interrogator offered them food, spoke to them respectfully, and addressed their needs... many—not all—suddenly came to our side. When their preconceived beliefs, their indoctrinated beliefs, were shown to be false... their pattern was broken, and they were left with a host of other emotions.

Everything a person experiences in life comes first and foremost by their expectations of what they think will happen. This decides on whether or not they are in a good mood or a bad mood. Whether or not they trust someone or watch them like a hawk. And with that understanding, it also means that when these things are subverted, people's brains are forced to do a reboot, change what they expect, their patterns shifted or broken... their minds open to new suggestions.

Pattern interrupts do not have a system, they do not have a process, and they are done simply by subverting the expectations of others. However, you do that. Whether you bang your hand on a table unexpectedly to immediately grab someone's attention or you make a funny face for no reason to make someone laugh. When you subvert the expectations of a person, you immediately drop them into a trance-like state for a few seconds. What you can do in those few seconds is up to you. Some people use it to do amazing things. Other people let it pass on by. But in the end, you will be able to work with people on a completely different level.

WARM HOT AND COLD READING

Cold reading is the tool of the psychic and the charlatan, but it is a very effective tool of the charlatan and psychic. It also creates an important skill, which is the art of inductive and deductive reasoning. If you have ever watched an episode of Sherlock or the Mentalist, you have seen these men on television put together an entire knowledge of a person. This is a real ability, though made flashy on television that is not inescapable for the average human. Each of these methods of reading people is important to understand because it will increase your ability to interact and engage with others powerfully and straightforwardly.

Cold reading relies on taking general problems people have, like money, love, and family, and asking broad questions to take their answers to as close to a yes as possible. What do I mean by that? The purpose of cold reading is not that you make statements that are 100% correct, but, rather, that you ask questions that get you to statements, based on what they say, that feels 100% correct. Questions like, "I would say you're having a problem at your home?" This sounds like a direct statement, right. In truth, what does home mean? What makes a home? So they say, "No, my house is fine...." And you can respond with, "I don't mean your physical home, but isn't something's bothering you that's disrupting your life?" They can think about it, and odds are, there is always something, so they say yes. "And that effect on your life, it can feel like it's affecting other things right?" Each step of the way, it is simply a process of asking questions that turn No's into Maybes and maybe's into yes and yes into amazing. When you add cold reading into active listening and understanding a person better than they understand themselves, you transform the way they will experience you and think of you.

Warm and Hot Reading are just a variation of cold reading, where you research the person ahead of time. That is all. The more information you can have on someone the more information you can use to read and understand them. There is nothing mysterious about that process, simply a structure of investigating people and using that information to better understand them.

PARTS THERAPY

Finally, let us get to an advanced tool when working with clients or yourself with hypnosis. Our personalities are not linear; rather we are usually an amalgam of different parts. If you are overweight, there is a part of you that wants to lose weight, slim down, feel great, and there is a part of you that wants to eat whatever you want. These two parts conflict with each other and thus you face the challenges you face and the struggles that keep you from being completely free of your struggles. Parts therapy is a process of fixing all of that, by helping people and you work on and transform each part, addressing the needs and challenges that each part presents of yourself.

This is done by having a person identify the parts of them that conflict. This can be hard for people, because, as much as they know they need help or want help, they sometimes are still pressed with the difficulty of understanding what causes their problem. It is one thing to understand that you have a problem, another thing to understand the cause of it. That is what parts therapy draws its strength from. It helps people identify the routes of their problem so they can better face it and deal with it.

So how do you do it?

- One isolates the part that needs work.
- Two, find out what motivates this part of them to take the actions it takes.
- Three, have them thank the part of them that has been taking this action, as it has been doing it for them as some form of benefit that they have been reaping all this time.

- Four, have them let go of the old behavior and that part of them and replace it with the part of them that wants the change.
- Five, have them search for the part of them that once wanted the negative behavior. If they still find it... repeat the process.

This simple five-step process, done while the person is under hypnosis, can truly transform the way they deal with their problems, and with themselves. It is a powerful tool that really and completely changes lives.

YOUR MASTERY IS JUST BEGINNING

Look, I understand that there has been a ton of stuff thrown at you. Techniques that you might feel you only got the brunt end of when it comes to understanding them and using them. But it is okay. The great thing about hypnosis is that the hypnotist should develop the methodology that works best for them. What I have tried to do, and I hope I have succeeded in giving you a basic understanding of how all these techniques work. What underlies their major functions, and how you can use them?

Hypnosis takes years to master but can be learned in a day. This basic bit of information are the building blocks needed to use hypnosis and do something with it if you do want to. Whether it is a parlor trick with friends, or it has to help, someone stop smoking. You have hopefully been able to discern a host of techniques that can generate results when it comes to hypnosis.

Chapter 14: How Hypnosis Fits Into Therapy

MANY PROBLEMS HAPPEN WITH A NON-CONSCIOUS PATTERN

All psychological and some physical difficulties involve trance states. A trance state involves a narrowing focus of attention. When a client comes to you with a problem, they rarely see multiple perspectives and when they do, they don't see them as something they could overcome. All problem patterns involve some level of trance. In a trance, you get a bias of perception. A depressed person looks at reality negatively and past orientated, for example, compared to an optimistic person who looks at reality positively and future-orientated.

Most hypnotic techniques and skills are designed to break the client free from problem trances and create multiple perspectives. Sometimes it can be best to encourage the problem rather than fight it. This can help to maintain and build rapport and can also misdirect the client from recognizing that what you are suggesting is actually what creates the solution.

The main reasons for problems are:

• Emotional needs not being met

- Harmful or unrealistic expectations
- Faulty pattern matching
- Feeling overwhelmed
- Worrying
- Developing a problem behavior pattern
- Being unable to break out of a trance state

Most problems involve people getting themselves into double binds (damned if you do, damned if you don't), or lacking certain skills or abilities (to relax or to build rapport, etc.) or finding themselves experiencing splitting or linking. Splitting is where you don't want to carry out the problem behavior and yet you carry out the problem anyway, this is a trance problem – your conscious awareness is that you don't want to do something, or you want to behave in one way, and yet, non-consciously the undesired response is what is activated leading to the problem behavior occurring whether you consciously wanted it to or not.

HOW HYPNOSIS FITS INTO THERAPY

Hypnosis isn't therapy, hypnosis is just about communication. There is a lot of confusion among the general public about what hypnotherapy is, many think hypnotherapists all do something called hypnotherapy and that it doesn't matter who you go to because they will all be doing about the same type of therapy.

All counselors, psychotherapists, cognitive-behavioral therapists, or any other psychological therapist will be doing hypnosis as part of what they do, they will be guiding and narrowing their clients' focus of attention. It could be a counselor reflecting what a client has just said for the client to continue focusing down that path of thinking, or reflecting "what do you think?" This encourages the client to narrow their focus, journey inside their mind further to think more about what they are discussing, and to try to find an answer. It could be a therapist encouraging a client to follow thoughts and memories back towards a root memory or cause where the problem first occurred. It could be a cognitive-behavioral therapist asking a client to think about their thinking, or a solution-focused therapist encouraging a client to imagine what life would be like if they didn't have the presenting problem. All of these are examples of doing hypnosis, but most therapists who do these things don't think of them as doing hypnosis and often know very little about it, having likely never taken any training in hypnosis.

The difference between these therapists doing hypnosis and a hypnotherapist doing hypnosis is that the hypnotherapist has more training and so often understands how to do it more effectively than the average therapist.

How hypnosis fits into therapy, is that it is used to encourage a favorable state of learning in the client and to facilitate the periods of inner work. It is often used to guide someone into a relaxed, yet alert state, to allow them to do effective mental rehearsal altering memories and practicing future behaviors. This is done based on the therapeutic work that has been undertaken using whatever therapeutic approach the therapist is trained to use.

Hypnotic Relaxation

Hypnotic relaxation is not hugely different from what you experience when you lay down after a long day, except that it has directed and controlled. I know that does not sound relaxing, but, in truth, when done correctly, people oftentimes have not experienced the level of relaxation they get, when you are putting them into a hypnotic relaxed state.

Hypnotic relaxation is all about focusing the mind into a single point, and thus being able to let go of those things. People can start getting itchy, scratching themselves, and bringing them out of their relaxed state. Sometimes, more times, than you would expect, people start to cry, or their eyes will start to water. This again is because the body is so used to holding everything back, but when they truly let go and let their bodies completely relax; emotions start to pour to the surface.

So, how does one induce hypnotic relaxation?

First and foremost, it is about following along with James Braid's first observation of induction. Fixation of vision and thought. Whether you have them stare at a spot on the wall, they stare in your eyes, or they look at a swinging watch, you want them focused, and listening to your voice.

Second, you want to guide them into deep breathing. Taking deep breaths in and slowly blowing them out through pursed lips.

After that, you want to walk them through their bodies, from their toes to their heads, having them focus on relaxing every bit of their body along the way. As they focus on every part of their body, they focus on releasing any stress, tension, or anxiety that is kept in those muscles. Some use a process of progressive relaxation, where they have the subject tighten their muscles for a few seconds and then relax them, tighten and then relax, all the way up and down the body and then the whole body. Either/or (or both) can work to help people completely get into a relaxed state.

Trance

Trance is a hard thing to nail down, as it is more a term used for hypnosis, rather than an actual medical state that one enters. For this write-up though, let us consider trance to be any state of hyperactive relaxation, focus, or confusion, for which a person becomes highly suggestible, loses track of time, and/or becomes unaware of their surroundings. Yes, I know that is a pretty broad status of what trance could be. But, in truth, life is in large ways a trance that we walkthrough. Often, we are left making decisions for things based on experiences we had as children, even when those experiences are no longer relevant to us as adults. If you are trying to help people with hypnosis, you will find this to be largely the case for many problems that people face. It is not that they are stuck in childhood, but, rather, they have a suggestion stuck in their mental programming that keeps playing out repeatedly, and they respond each time as if they have a post-hypnotic suggestion and they just enter a trance state and act without consciousness.

Trance might not be easily defined, but, when you know what to look for, it becomes pretty easy to recognize and utilize. Ever get into a conversation with someone and you watch their pupils dilate, their attention focused solely on you as you focus solely on them, and the rest of the world just begins to fall away and disappear. Ever start driving down the road and end up in your driveway not sure how you got there and a little worried that you do not know. And have you ever just sat down, watched a good show, and looked up to realize the entire day has disappeared? I know I have asked these questions before, but they bear repeating, because each of these times, your brain had entered a trance state.

When you have a person fixate on a single point, whether it's the long road in front of them, or it's a television screen, or a wall, or a watch, all those thoughts they have can start to get pushed aside, and they can start to lose themselves in the focus. As they enter a trance state, you can begin to use the state and guide people deeper into the trance state.

All trances have certain depths to them. Traditional hypnosis, for the most part, likes to work on a moderate hypnotic trance, this is where people are fairly ambulatory, responsive, and focused. Light trance is what we are in all day long. We are awake, for the most part, but, we are not completely free of our past decisions and thoughts. Rather, we make decisions based on our old programming and hope for the best.

When we are completely asleep, it is itself a form of trance, where you put the focus on going to sleep and you let your mind rest. As you enter from one level of hypnotic depth to another, from groggy to dead asleep, each of these things has powerful effects on the body, the mind, and the thinking.

Though there is work that can be done on each level of trance, the only thing you need to focus on is the most basic level for almost all the hypnotic work you could be doing. And that basic trance state is simple fixation and following directions.

Eye Fixation

As people have gotten relaxed, they have not fully entered into a trance yet. They have simply gotten their body and mind into a more receptive place for them to completely begin to listen to you and accept what you have to say and what you want to tell them. So, as you would transition from having someone relax, you would request them to gently open their eyes. Now that they are fully relaxed, you would keep them fixated on whatever point they started at. As they fixate on that point, you can begin to use hypnotic suggestions to guide them into greater levels of trance.

You might be wondering why someone fixating on a single point becomes more susceptible to suggestion. What you need to understand is that exactly what I pointed out in earlier chapters about our conscious brain being able to only take in a few bits of information. When a person fixates on a single point, most of that conscious mind is taken up by that act alone. They are then left with listening and following your directions, especially once they have entered a relaxed state, and have let go of the stresses and worries they have had in the past.

Fractionation

As you guide people in and out of their trance state, this is a process called fractionation. In fractionation, it creates a slingshot effect that brings people deeper and deeper into a trance, every time they go back into it.

Fractionation allows you to take people into deeper levels of trance and make them more comfortable with the trance process. Like most things, going deep into trance is not a linear path that the brain just walks itself through. Instead, it is a powerful process that occasionally a person needs a break from, a chance to respond and willfully go deeper.

But, the huge benefit of taking a person in and out of a trance is the ability to test your hypnotic suggestions, make sure they are responding, and each time, and make it easier and easier for them to be your perfect hypnotic subject.

Fractionation can be a very powerful tool for people that struggle to go into trance or struggle to focus and go along with you. This may seem counter-intuitive, but, remember, as we said, everyone lives in trance at some point and time in their lives. So the problem rarely is that a person is not being hypnotized, or is not entering a trance state, but, rather that they have not entered the trance state you need them to.

The more people begin to follow along with what you want them to do, the easier it will be for them to hear you and follow along. If they can follow your directions, they will eventually be able to enter into a trance state easier and easier and be more receptive to your process of doing it. Most hypnotists miss this point and think that a person simply cannot be hypnotized, or that they are not the personality to be hypnotized. But this just is not true.

Fractionation is also the key to embedding hypnotic suggestions on different levels of the unconscious mind. By this, I mean, that the suggestions you give to people in a hypnotic state can better embed if they are layered on top of each other, building a perfect pyramid transformation.

Guided Visualization

Visualization is one of the most important techniques when it comes to hypnosis. As you guide people through their trance state, helping them to envision the changes you want them to make, or, as you will see with the arm levitation technique, having them imagine certain things going on with their body, you can use images and imagination to help them transform.

Using imagery and visualization is a necessary part of all hypnosis and for a lot of people who are not using the script; it is a difficult part of hypnosis. It can be hard sometimes to create the proper imagery, to guide people down the stairway of their unconscious, to unlock the door, and enter the room of their mind, to travel through the room, or go outside, and see the stream of their unconscious mind, pour delicately from the fountains of change that they are searching for.

The thing is that most people when you talk with them will give you a large amount of the imagery that you need to use to help them truly get what they want from their hypnosis. But, if you are not going by a script, then you can expect to work on your hypnotic language, by simply looking around at the world around you and attempting to describe it more vividly. Think of a scene, describe things out loud, and then describe it into a recorder. Do it slowly, use your voice dynamically to describe things, as if you are trying to draw people into listening to every word you have to say? As you do this, you will get better and better at using hypnotic language to the best of your ability.

Once you learn how to use hypnotic imagery and description to guide the mind, things become a lot easier for you to do.

Body Scan

People hold emotions throughout their bodies. Just as we pointed out about people fully relaxing for the first time, they can find themselves crying and their body having a reaction that tries to pull them from their trance. When you successfully have guided a person into the early stages of trance and begin to help them with what they want to be solved. Whether it is to stop smoking, or lose weight, or stop stressing, or whatever else they may be experiencing that they want hypnosis to help with. You want them to find it in their bodies first.

Where does that need for that cigarette to arise? Is it in their lungs? Is it on the back of their tongue? Is it on their fingers? They need to scan their bodies and figure out where these sensations begin. Because as much as we are psychological creatures, we are physical as well. And the major way to change anything psychologically is to also make sure you alter the physical form as well.

Think about it for a moment, if you have not before. Where does your head go when you are sad? Where does it go when you are happy? Are your shoulder slumped forward or pulled back when you are feeling good? Your body knows all the techniques for all your emotional states and it will do its best to get you there to help you achieve that state.

The body scan lets people analyze their body and find all their hidden emotional spots so that they can be pulled deeper and deeper into their hypnotic state, and better transform their state so that they can get the change they want.

When you take people through this process, you set them up for other things as well, such as the hypnotic phenomenon.

Arm Levitation and other Basic Hypnotic Phenomenon

You have probably witnessed some basic hypnotic phenomena. Each of these is powerful in helping convince the person that they have been hypnotized and to see how hypnotized they are. The three phenomena we will talk about and I will give you the basic scripts for right now are the Arm Levitation, Hands Stuck Together, and The Closing Fingers.

Let us start with the closing fingers technique. This one is really fun to do and you can do it anywhere with very little prep. A person does not need to be hypnotized, but, rather, they need to simply follow direction, and focus. It is a great way to show them that their mind can follow directions and that they can be hypnotized.

Here is what happens. You tell a person to put their hands together, rub them together, and then interlace their fingers together, gripping them tightly together. Then tell them to take their pointer fingers and stick them up, while their hands stay together, and them apart and separate, and stare into the space between them. As they stare into the space between their fingers, you tell them to imagine a magnet that pulls their fingers together. Slowly, their fingers will draw together until they are connected. Once their fingers connect, tell them to put their hands into their lap and relax.

Now, there are suggestions you can give them. "The more you look at the space between your fingers, the smaller and smaller it gets, as your fingers get closer and closer together. You can try and resist and though you may jerk your fingers apart, they're constantly being drawn together again and again."

Chapter 15: Hypnotherapy (How to induce a trance in someone)

Hypnotism is often confused with spiritualism or is considered to be an aspect of the supernatural. This is not true. Hypnotism deals with mental strength and focusing that energy to obtain results. Whether you wish to hypnotize others or simply benefit from subconscious reprogramming yourself. The fact is that our subconscious – the part of us that we are not aware of in our waking state – is the most important part of our mind.

It is the subconscious that truly controls what we do, that gives us our urges, our willpower, our desires, and sometimes our weaknesses. It is the subconscious that holds on to that fear of spiders or that fear of crowds. It is that subconscious that tells you that eating will assuage your stress or anger. It is that subconscious that is addicted to cigarettes or alcohol, or that is unable to let go of the chronic pain in your life. And it is the subconscious that is your key to a better life, the key to letting go of destructive habits and improving your attitudes, behaviors, and thus life.

CHOOSING THE SUBJECT

The first step in hypnotizing anybody is to find a person who is interested in getting hypnotized. If you are just starting, it is imperative to find someone willing to get hypnotized. Ensure you tell the person you choose everything that you will do in detail. Gain the confidence of the person by communicating with them and making them comfortable. At the end of the day, they should be confident in your abilities and comfortable enough. They should also feel that they are in safe hands, as this will produce better results. When choosing someone, also choose someone patient and relaxed about the whole procedure. Do not try to hypnotize someone without their consent. Do not exercise your skills on people with disorders especially mental disorders. Hypnotism focuses on the mind and people with any mental illness could get aggravated leading to severe and complicated problems.

Most people have very skewed views on hypnotism. This is due to inadequate light that is thrown on this art form through mediums like fiction books, movies, and TV shows. Hypnosis is a technique that is used to relax the minds of the people. It provides insightfulness and clarity to the person. It also reduces brain fog and eradicates stress that comes with pondering over problems in the subconscious. Hypnotism is something we undergo every day. The term 'spacing out' is pretty much what hypnotism is all about and we go into these via dreams as well. It is important to tell the person you will hypnotize that they won't go into a sleep-induced form or become unconscious. Hypnotized people still have control over themselves and are not in someone else's control. Hypnosis has several benefits including reducing anxiety and increasing metabolism. It makes the mind more powerful by making it more focused and sharper. It also increases concentration and is a relaxation technique. It is best to find out the reasons why your partner wants to get hypnotized. This will reduce ambiguity and you can comply with his or her request. It also gives you a chance to know them well and get an insight into their thought process. This makes it easier to get them into the trance-like state.

Also, make it a point to ask them about any prior experience that they have had with regard to hypnotism. Find out their opinions and views on this art as well. If they have been hypnotized before you can find out about how responsive they were and what makes them uncomfortable. You can avoid the things that they don't want to do and opt for alternate techniques. You can also gauge the partner and person you are dealing with. It is also easier to hypnotize someone who has been hypnotized before. Be sure to reassure your subject. They should trust you and believe in what you do. Guide them gently and be prepared to answer all of their questions.

Apart from choosing a subject to hypnotize, also choose a good location. The place that you choose must be free of distractions; it must be clean and quiet. It must also be comfortable. Remove distractive items like TVs, music systems and shut all windows if there is lots of noise. Switch off all phones and alarms. Close the door and ensure the lights are dim. It is important to note that the room should not be dingy and dark. Also, ensure it is just you and your subjects. Let them sit in a comfortable position in a chair.

EASE THEM INTO A TRANCE LIKE STATE

Make them feel comfortable and once they are in a comfortable position, ask them to close their eyes. Speak in a slow and calm voice. Keep your voice leveled and soothing. Drawl your sentences to make them sound smooth and talk like you are trying to calm someone. Speak softly and clearly. It is important to keep this soft mellow tone throughout the entire hypnosis session. Ask them to get into the zone by thinking of happy experiences. Alternately you can also start by asking them to imagine themselves in a peaceful location. A lush garden or a peaceful meadow or anything calming and serene. Talk like how you would talk to a child and make it a point to periodically reassure them. Request them rather than command them. Tell them that they are in control and that they are safe. Also, give them their space and time to comply with your requests and suggestions. Ask them to relax and breathe deeply. Ask them to concentrate and focus on an aspect and breathe in and out deeply and slowly. Let them be in charge of their breathing. It is a good idea to also support them in this endeavor by matching their breathing to yours. Give clear-cut instructions for instance "Take a deep breath and hold it for a few seconds, now slowly let it out". Spend a moment or two on getting their breathing organized. This will give clarity and focus due to the high oxygen content that will go to the subject's brain.

If you prefer working with your subject with their eyes open, then simply ensure that they concentrate or focus on a particular point. Let them look and fix their gaze at either you or something else in the room. Wait for a moment until they are concentrating completely on the object. Make it a point to keep your gaze focused on them as well. This will let you know whether their concentration or focus is wavering. You can also offer guidance when they become distracted and gently bring them back to the stage of focus. Ask them to focus and pay attention. Tell them to also relax their eyelids.

When it comes to relaxing they must relax their body part by part. Make sure they are calm and that they are breathing properly. Start by gently instructing them to relax their feet. Ask them to leave these muscles freely and relax them. From here keep moving upwards like their calves, their thighs, their torso, back, arms, shoulders, neck, and finally face. When doing this keep your voice calm and gentle. Also do not rush them and give them ample time to relax. Speak encouraging words and give reassurance when need be. It is important that they are relaxed and that they are comfortable.

Keep an eye out on the subject's body language and breathing. This will give you an insight into their mental condition. The goal at this stage is to ensure that your subject is completely relaxed. If they still seem stiff and uncertain, use soothing words, pleasant imagery, and even use soothing songs to calm them. Look for any signs for fidgeting and twitching like darting of the eyes, wriggling of toes, tapping of fingers, and so on. If they do have signs of these, then encourage them to get them to relax. Alternately you can also have a pleasing fragrance like incense sticks that will help them reach the relaxed state a lot faster.

Once they are completely at ease and have relaxed, you can start by inducing thoughts. You can opt for using the 'hypnotic staircase' technique. This technique is a very popular technique that is often used by hypnotists and hypnotherapies. It enables one to get into the trance-like state. Ask them to imagine themselves standing on top of a staircase. Then ask them to envision them walking down step by step. Each step will make them relax and they sink further into the trance-like state. The subject will get more absorbed in himself or herself. Use a soothing, controlled voice for this purpose. Ask them to relax after each step by giving them clear instructions, for instance, "You are on top of a long staircase, you will start walking down this staircase and with each step you will relax. Take the first step and you will feel your body relaxing, now slowly step down on the second step, you will feel your mind becoming calm." Ensure that they become perfectly relaxed and are a trance-induced state by the end of this exercise. You can also induce thoughts by making them walk into happy surroundings and a happy place. Give them more details and describe the scenarios well so that they can picture these in their mind's eye. Also, it enables them to imagine. As they slip further into the trance-like state, ask them simple descriptive questions. Ask them what color the flowers of the garden are, what color clothes they are wearing and so on. You will be able to picture what is happening in their mind through this exercise and after a point, you will no longer just be asking questions but helping them to focus their imagination and create vivid colors and shapes. Also, ask them what they are seeing around them, and when you get good descriptive answers you know that they are in the trance-like state.

At this point start to opt for a more commanding tone. Keep your voice light and soothing but once they have reached the trance-like states make your voice more assertive and instructive. Instead of requesting start to command, opt to use words such as "Do this" instead of "Could you do this". At these points, they will start responding to you and adhering to your words. They should be able to respond to what you are asking and carrying out tasks that you instruct them on. It is important to not question them on personal aspects or anything they wouldn't be comfortable sharing. Also, when they are in the trance-like state use positive and encouraging words to maintain that state. Keep a goal in mind and adhere to that goal. Be sure to provide positivity.

HAVE A GOAL IN MIND

Hypnotize someone with good intentions. Ensure you have a goal in mind. Chances are the person you are hypnotizing will remember what they were instructed to do or say. It is for this reason you shouldn't violate any ethical code. Ask them to do simple tasks and answer regular questions that they would be happy to answer even if they weren't hypnotized. Do not use hypnosis to prank someone. Hypnosis is an art form that is used for positive purposes. For instance, you can use hypnosis to reduce your subject's anxiety levels. You don't even have to instruct your subjects or make them carry out any task. Making them come into this trance-like state is proven to reduce stress levels and give them clarity. This is because of the deep relaxation they feel when they are in this trance-like state. Know that you can't fix any problem or solve anything, but you can ease their tensions. If the subject has any particular problem, then you can ask them to envision solutions. You can get them to solve their problems instead of spoon-feeding them. For instance, if they are worried about their future, you can ask them to envision a brighter future; you can ask them simple questions that would induce solutions.

If they do have bigger problems and ones that you, as a beginner cannot solve, it is better to ask them to go to a specialist or go to a hypnotherapist. If they are suffering from severe addictions, mental trauma, self-esteem issues, and so on, it is better to recommend them to a trained medical professional. If, however, it is mild and you are trying to get them to stop something, for instance, you are trying to get them to quit smoking. Then you can use encouraging words in the trance-like state enabling them to quit smoking. Help them imagine a world without their addiction using positive words, good imagery, and soothing tones. It is also a good idea to know the goal of the subject and why he or she wants to get hypnotized. You can modify your technique appropriately.

Hypnotherapy is a relaxing technique. It combines focus and relaxation for optimum results. You must note that hypnosis is not something that is done to fix problems. It is allowing the subject to muse over their problem and fixes it in their own accord. You, as a hypnotist only serves as a medium towards this. Do not expect immediate results. It is a slow and steady process and can only be done with the willingness of your subject. Since it uses a lot of mind power and self-reflection and introspection, it is advisable to hypnotize someone with a balanced mind. If they require major help it is best to direct them to a professional.

COMPLETING THE HYPNOSIS

It is important to slowly take them out of their trance-like state. Do not pronounce sudden movements and instructions. Let them slowly come out of the hypnotic state and become aware of the surrounding. The ideal way to do this is to tell them gently that you will count till a stipulated number after which they will be out of their trance-like state. When doing this, give adequate pauses of at least a second between each count. This will induce awareness. Alternately you can guide them back upstairs with each step they take making them more aware. When doing this explain to them that they will get more pronounced and alert in a soothing manner. Give them time to settle down and focus their thoughts once they have woken up. Do not engage them in heavy conversation or ask them to do any exciting or exhausting tasks, this will lead to disorientation and brain fog.

When they seemed to have relaxed and become steady, you can opt for simple conversations. Be encouraging and tell them that they did well. Also, discuss the hypnosis with them. Ask them their thoughts and opinions, how they felt, how the experience was, and so on. This will help you understand your technique a lot better and you will be able to gauge your impact on a person. It will also give you an insight into the experience of the person and provide you with corrective measures and steps to make yourself better at hypnosis. Don't pressurize anybody and give them adequate time to collect their thoughts. Also, if they want to be left alone, comply with their request. Be prepared to answer all their questions with an open mind.

ANSWER ALL QUERIES

You are likely to experience a huge volume of questions after you are done with the hypnosis. At this point, it is best to answer them honestly. Be mentally prepared to answer all the questions and clarify any doubts. The subject is likely to have questions before and after the hypnosis is done. The main reason behind preparation is to gain the confidence and trust of the subject. If the person is reluctant and untrusting towards you then he or she will not respond positively or comply with your commands. The questions that you are likely to be asked and the possible answers you can give are discussed below.

Is this all-safe?

Absolutely. In no way am I going to change you. You will not be forced into doing or saying anything you don't want to. You will be in charge and I will be your guide. You will experience the focus and precision of your subconscious. You will experience relaxation and soothing sensation. It is perfectly safe and after it is done you will be back to the same person.

What is your course of action?

It is very simple. I will request you to carry out some simple commands that you will comply with even when you are not in the trance-like state. You have the power to refuse and reject anything I say or ask of you. You are in control of yourself and you will be able to come out of the trance-like state by yourself. I will simply ask you to imagine or envision some scenes and ask you to narrate what you are seeing through your mind's eye.

How does it feel to be hypnotized?

Hypnotism is something where you will get induced into a trance-like state. This is very common especially when we sleep because dreams have a similar ability to make us go into this trance-like state. Hypnosis will help you focus your thoughts, give you clarity, and help you to relax your mind. It also increases your concentration and enhances brain metabolism. It is very similar to altering your consciousness when you watch a good TV show or hear a lovely musical piece. When you are so focused and into something, you will view it from a different perspective. For instance, when you are watching a movie, you get so absorbed by it you start viewing it from a different perspective rather than just being a part of the audience. This is precisely how being hypnotized feels.

Will you make me do things or say things that I don't want to?

No. When you are hypnotized you are still in control of yourself. Your personality or your mind doesn't get altered. You can reject anything you don't want to do and not respond if you don't want to answer something. You are in control of yourself and you wouldn't do anything that you don't normally do.

What are some ways through which I can be more responsive?

The easiest way through which you can respond a lot better is through relaxing. You will be absorbed into yourself. You will be focusing a lot harder and explore the power of your subconscious. If you are willing to comply and if you are eager to experience it then you will respond a lot better. If you focus and relax and let yourself loose and allow the hypnotizer to guide you, then you will be able to experience the effects of hypnotism a lot better.

Is it possible that there are cases where I don't want to come back?

The suggestions that the hypnotizer will give you and the various instructions are simply exercised for the mind. You are delving deeper into your subconscious. You will be in control of yourself and responsible for your actions. Once the hypnotism session is over you will be more aware and you will return to a normal state of mind. It is a state of deep relaxation and when this happens you might not want to come back, but you can't do much in the hypnotic state. The hypnotizer will also try to bring you back. You can also be brought back by yourself during emergency cases.

Are there cases where hypnotism will not work?

There are most certainly cases where hypnotism will take a longer time to work on some people but generally, everybody can get hypnotized. Imagine instances where you are so absorbed in something that you don't hear what is happening around you or imagining a situation where you will have to wake up early and manage to wake up the next day. All these are instances that show that there are so many hidden abilities that we can do with our brains and that it is powerful beyond measure. Some of us have managed to develop our minds and tune it in a certain manner to help us go about our tasks. Usually, people who haven't been hypnotized before have a hard time getting hypnotized due to enthusiasm, apprehension, and other emotions that do not let them relax completely. However, if you focus and relax and let yourself be guided by the hypnotizer you will get hypnotized a lot sooner. If you also actively participate and follow instructions of the hypnotizer, you will be able to find success.

If we only use our imagination in this task, how is it beneficial?

Hypnotism uses and channels your imagination into focusing and concentrating. It provides a platform for visualization and imagery. It makes your mind more creative as it exercises the brain and increases the efficiency of it. The mind is very strong as it controls every other part of our body, it is also the organ with which we think, make decisions and through proper training, we can unleash our mental potential. Hypnotism enables us to achieve this.

Chapter 16: Self-Hypnosis

Self-hypnosis is one of the most powerful things people can do for themselves. It can be transformative and change the way they relate to themselves and their problems. For the longest time, many hypnotists have disagreed with the idea of self-hypnosis. Believing that people need a directive voice to guide them down the path of their unconscious mind. However, that is just not true. There are several ways you can use self-hypnosis to improve your life, create amazing results for yourself, and heal yourself of problems.

First and foremost are the NLP techniques that we talked about. From the Swish Pattern to Reframing, they are both powerful tools of self-hypnosis that allow you to alter your state, and powerfully use your hypnosis. You can train your mind and alter your horizons.

Self-Hypnosis can be difficult to get used to, but, when you know what you are doing, you can do it quickly and easily.

RECORD YOUR OWN TRANCE

You have learned how to induce hypnosis and create a trance. One of the fastest ways to create a powerful self-hypnotic state is to simply record your voice and guide yourself through the process so that you can create a powerful hypnotic process. I know this might feel like an extra step to something you will be able to do by yourself, but it is important to know what you can do. Simply take the recorder from your phone, record a hypnotic session, and bring yourself into a trance and use that process to enter a state of self-hypnosis.

CREATE A HYPNOTIC ANCHOR

Before NLP and before Hypnosis was used around the world, there was Ivan Pavlov who was investigating the digestive system through measurements of the salivation in dogs. While he was doing this, he noticed something strange happening. Eventually, he noticed that the dogs seemed to salivate before the food even came. He thought at first it was psychic salivation. However, the answer was a little more obvious and worldly, and it was that the bell that he set up to remember to feed the dogs on schedules had conditioned the dogs. Every time the bell rang, the dog is expected to be fed and began to salivate so they could better eat the food. The bell became an anchor.

Anchoring uses external stimuli to trigger internal states. It does not matter what state you want to summon. If you want to feel confident, ease your stress, stop feeling angry, or just focus better. Anchoring gives you a powerful tool giving you an arsenal to take better control over your emotions.

Imagine being able to simply and easily press your fingers together to ease a craving for anything that once was a hurdle to not surrender to. Imagine, taking control of your anger and immediately making yourself calm and relaxed at a snap of the fingers. Just imagine how amazing and powerful it could be to be able to turn stress into energy. Imagine, taking sadness and turn it into creativity. Creating anchors can transform your life and transform the way you live your life. You will be empowered and most importantly be in control of your life in a way you have never been before.

You do not need to have a difficult or challenging life. You deserve to have an amazing life. But if you do not have control over your emotions, everything can feel really difficult, and hard.

Let us get down to how to make a powerful anchor for anything and everything you want in your life.

THE PROCESS

Let us remember back to when we talked about visualization and how your brain cannot tell the difference from an imagined event and the actual event. That is pretty important to understanding everything that will happen. This is important for this process. More important when it comes to anchoring than imagining actions, you want to imagine emotions. You want to let your body feel the emotion you want, feel everything in your body that you would feel when you have that emotion. Whatever emotion you want to feel, whether it is happy, excited, focus, or confident, you know how these feelings feel, and how your body will feel when you are in that state. The more vivid you can create that emotion, the better you will be.

So, let us get to the process of creating a powerful anchor that will transform your life.

Figure out the Emotion You Want

Look inside yourself and figure out what emotion will serve you. Figure out what emotion will best give you the motivation and energy you need for whatever state you want to conjure.

Imagine That Emotion to the Fullest

Once you have a clear image of what that emotion is, you need to imagine that emotion to the fullest extent. What does that mean? It means you have to understand how that emotion will play out in your body, in your mind, and your life. How does your body position itself? Imagine each emotion to the fullest.

At the Peak Of Emotion Create an Anchor

At the peak of your emotional state, you need to create the anchor that will be able to activate that emotion. You can clap your hands together, squeeze some fingers together, stomp your feet, bite your tongue, whatever you need to do, you want to create a physical stimulus that you can connect to your emotional state. Each anchor should be individualized to the emotions that you want. And you want to make sure that when you make the anchor, you make it at the peak of your emotional strength.

Reinforce It

When you have made the anchor, you need to reinforce it. The process of reinforcing the anchor involves you fractionating from the state, and then getting back into the state. So, you want to get your mind out of your emotional state, by altering your physical state. Whether you do some jumping jacks, or some push-ups, or whatever you need to break the state. Then sit back down, bring back the emotion, and anchor it again. Repeat this process two or three times, until you start to feel it, and know that it is being anchored.

Test the Anchor

Once you have worked your way through each step, you want to clear your mind again by breaking your state and then testing the anchor to see that it is working. Look for any signs that you are experiencing the emotions as they come. Remember, you will need to do this multiple times to make it permanent. But, on your first time, you should be able to feel some emotion tied to it.

If you are working this process by yourself, it will take you more time, but you can build these results. As you do this, you will discover things about your emotional life and your emotional world. As you go through the process and create the anchors you will find new freedom and new power in your emotional control. You will also discover how your body creates emotions and how your body forms emotions, giving you a greater understanding of your emotion. What does that mean?

After you have created a host of anchors for emotional states that you want to master, now's the time also to remember to use these processes to create a hypnotic state anchor. Whether you are using the recorded voice method, or one of the strategies that I will show you after this, by following the same procedure to create powerful anchors, you can create anchors for your hypnotic state. This will give you instant access to your unconscious mind and the ability to immediately maneuver your unconscious mind through self-hypnosis. The power of this anchor means that with a simple relaxed location, you will be able to enter a trance at will. This is the ideal way in which to practice self-hypnosis and the fastest way as well.

Of, course, the anchor needs to be built up to do it and that means that you need to be able to enter a hypnotic state to achieve it.

FIXATION, MANTRAS, AND LONG BOUT MEDITATION

Self-Hypnosis can be achieved through a process of fixation and mantras. This may sound new age, or religious, but it is not. The process of using meditation to enter a state of self-hypnosis is well documented, though of course, it is a bit challenging, as any form of self-hypnosis can be.

But, let us give it ago. Focus on the wall in front of you or on the ceiling if you are laying down. Relax. Let your body go loose and let your eyes begin to blur. As you do this, steady your breathing, and bring your thoughts to your breathing. In and out, slow and steady, each breath deep and filling. As you do this, let your body relax even more.

Once you feel completely relaxed, take a deep breath in, and then blow out fully, and shut your eyes. Here, you will think of your unconscious, whatever it might be. For most, it is a room. For some, it is a cave. For others, it is a den. It does not matter what it is, but, you will find it in your mind and you will enter it. As you enter it, you will then be able to walk yourself through the changes you want. This requires knowing what shifts you want to make and what changes you want to make before you do it. What metaphors are holding you back? What bright future do you want to achieve? Everything and anything you would walk someone through has to already be decided and put together, that you can place it together again in your unconscious.

Once it is there, you will test your state, repeatedly, to make sure that you have it right. You will look for any part of you that fights against these changes and address them in your self-induced state. Each of these things gives you the freedom to truly make your hypnotic state effective.

When you first enter that state, when you feel the complete relaxation flush through your body, using anchors for that moment can be very important and very helpful for the future. And with that, you have created a self-hypnotic state.

Self-hypnosis can be powerful, it can be wonderful, and it gives you the autonomy to make the changes that you want to make in your life, with or without anyone else. It is not difficult. But it will take time. The more you practice the better you will be in the end.

Conclusion

Hypnosis is still a mysterious thing, mainly because of the lack of knowledge most people have about what it is. But as treatment modalities have evolved, hypnosis or hypnotherapy has joined the ranks of suggested complementary techniques to improve areas in the human psyche that are resilient towards conventional treatments. Self-hypnosis has even paved the way for us to find our coping mechanisms, without the influence of outside forces. All these things have been made possible all because hypnosis takes the human subconscious and enhances how well we ought to approach suggestions – for improvement, for positive change, or daily life in general.

Training for successes in life is possible. With that said, self-hypnosis can be your ally, your go-to technique to help cope with the stressors in life, and to seek improvement. And the best thing about all this? Now is the time for you to make the best version of yourself you can be. So, go ahead and make it. Practice what you have learned and to help other people and yourself to live a happier, healthier, and more successful life through the power of suggestion.

The people who get the best results are those who take consistent action. Some techniques in this book will get the most immediate results, whereas others may require repetition and time to develop as any good skill does. Let these tools and skills provide you with a competitive advantage over other people. Some of the best communicators in the world use these skills and aren't aware of them, whereas others who are also great communicators are acutely aware of how and what they are communicating and to whom.

The tools that you learned in this book will provide you with the skills to influence those around you. These skills, when used consistently, will also help you reprogram your thoughts, your feelings, and your behaviors so you can live an even better life.

Start by picking one or two little things you can try and implement them. Then come back to this book again and again until you become the person you want to be. That person, who works well with others, wins others over to your side and keeps making progress in life until it's the way you've always envisioned it. Life's a journey, and we should work every day on becoming better at it.

So, go out there, take action, influence people, and have fun while doing it.

Go out into the world with fantastic new skills! The possibilities are limitless. The only limit, as they say, is your desire, dreams, and the intuitive drive to better yourself and the world around you and try new exciting new things. This skill could even take you to different parts of the world. Imagine visiting a faraway beach hotel in an exotic location to give a presentation and also have a chance to practice your hypnotic trade.

Lightning Source UK Ltd.
Milton Keynes UK
UKHW020048121220
374864UK00003B/302